"Ken Baum's approach is relentless, empowering and supportive."
—Sasha Cohen, U.S. Olympic figure skating champion

MIND
OVER
BUSINESS

How to Unleash Your Business
and Sales Success by Rewiring the
Mind/Body Connection

KEN BAUM

with Bob Andelman

PRENTICE HALL PRESS

PRENTICE HALL PRESS
Published by the Penguin Group
Penguin Group (USA) Inc.
375 Hudson Street, New York, New York 10014, USA
Penguin Group (Canada), 90 Eglinton Avenue East, Suite 700, Toronto, Ontario M4P 2Y3, Canada
(a division of Pearson Penguin Canada Inc.)
Penguin Books Ltd., 80 Strand, London WC2R 0RL, England
Penguin Group Ireland, 25 St. Stephen's Green, Dublin 2, Ireland (a division of Penguin Books Ltd.)
Penguin Group (Australia), 250 Camberwell Road, Camberwell, Victoria 3124, Australia
(a division of Pearson Australia Group Pty. Ltd.)
Penguin Books India Pvt. Ltd., 11 Community Centre, Panchsheel Park, New Delhi—110 017, India
Penguin Group (NZ), 67 Apollo Drive, Rosedale, Auckland 0632, New Zealand
(a division of Pearson New Zealand Ltd.)
Penguin Books (South Africa) (Pty.) Ltd., 24 Sturdee Avenue, Rosebank, Johannesburg 2196,
South Africa

Penguin Books Ltd., Registered Offices: 80 Strand, London WC2R 0RL, England

While the author has made every effort to provide accurate telephone numbers and Internet addresses at the time of publication, neither the publisher nor the author assumes any responsibility for errors or for changes that occur after publication. Further, the publisher does not have any control over and does not assume any responsibility for author or third-party websites or their content.

First edition: March 2012

Library of Congress Cataloging-in-Publication Data

Baum, Kenneth.
    Mind over business : how to unleash your business and sales success by rewiring the mind/body connection / Ken Baum with Bob Andelman.— 1st ed.
        p.   cm.
    ISBN 978-0-7352-0462-1
    1. Success in business.   2. Visualization.   3. Imagery (Psychology)   I. Andelman, Bob.   II. Title.
    HF5386.B2759   2011
    658.4'09—dc23   2011037120

PRINTED IN THE UNITED STATES OF AMERICA

10   9   8   7   6   5   4   3   2   1

Most Prentice Hall Press books are available at special quantity discounts for bulk purchases for sales promotions, premiums, fund-raising, or educational use. Special books, or book excerpts, can also be created to fit specific needs. For details, write: Special Markets, Penguin Group (USA) Inc., 375 Hudson Street, New York, New York 10014.

*To my mom, for teaching me the value of books
and research even though she had an eighth-grade education,
and my dad, for instilling a strong work ethic and
giving me one of the greatest gifts, an attitude
to do what needs to be done with what I have and not to
complain about what I don't.*

ACKNOWLEDGMENTS

Ken Baum

There are so many people that have influenced and provided insight into success that it would be impossible to mention them all. A few that stand out: Special thanks to the great business trainer Brian Tracy for inspiring and mentoring me early in my career. He lives what he teaches. And I will always be thankful for the legendary Zig Ziglar for his direction and critique that helped me become a better speaker. Ted Lang, founder of Equity Planning, first taught me how business works. I didn't appreciate it—or like it—at the time, but he was right. Action Speakers Bureau and National Seminars put me in the business circuit and trained me to be a high-content business trainer. Vic Conant of Nightingale-Conant produced my first audiobook.

My agents, Jane Dystel and Miriam Goderich at Dystel & Goderich Literary Management, do a great job for me every time out—and this is our third book project together. At Perigee/Prentice Hall Press, I am grateful to Maria Gagliano for her editing direction and patience. And speaking of which, this book wouldn't have happened without my coauthor, Bob Andelman, who showed the patience of Job and applied his many skills to bringing order to chaos as we put this together during the busiest, most exciting time of my life.

I also appreciate all of my clients and friends who provided the stories and insights that helped give the book life. Bill Walton for willingly sharing a personal challenge that is sure to inspire. Bill is one of the nicest, most sincere people I have ever met. Bob Bain, TV producer, husband and father who has raised three great kids and always has time for them, who took hours out of his busy schedule to contribute his story.

My kids, Bryce and Brittany, brighten my day every day. They followed their dreams and the path of the heart, rather than the path of convenience. I love you both more than anything else on earth.

And finally to the late Harlan Haupt, a truly good man who balanced family, work and religion and was as organized and efficient as anyone I have ever known—I miss you!

Onward and Upward!

Bob Andelman

Each book I write is the result of a unique set of partnerships, and *Mind Over Business* is no different. Thanks to my coauthor, Ken Baum, for an experience that was never dull and always memorable. (And we both say thanks to the staff at Luckie B's BBQ in St. Petersburg, Florida, for the delicious food and late-night supply of Dr. Pepper!)

Thanks to our editor, Maria Gagliano, for being understanding when deadlines slipped by a day (or three), and for offering terrific guidance in focusing and tightening the book's message and delivery.

I, too, am deeply indebted for the continued support of Jane Dystel, Miriam Goderich and Michael Bourret at Dystel & Goderich Literary Management. This book marks a decade of working together, and I appreciate every day of your support.

Becky James endured possibly the worst year of her life as Ken and I worked through the process of writing, but never failed to deliver transcriptions in a timely and accurate way. Thanks, Becky—things will only get better!

A special thanks to my 2010–11 middle school girls soccer team at Shorecrest Prep for letting me test a few of Ken's ideas on them and then being a good audience when Ken came to St. Petersburg to demonstrate Mindsetting and other exercises. (I bet they can still imagine the taste of that lemon!)

Finally, to my wife, Mimi, and daughter, Rachel: I always appreciate your willingness to work around my writing schedule and its always inconvenient demands. Love you both!

CONTENTS

INTRODUCTION

Imagine maximizing all of your education, all of your experience, and discovering latent talents you didn't know you had. Every day, I earn my living by guiding men and women to maximize their careers and potential. In this book, I'm going to share my unique knowledge and personally developed techniques with you. The Mind Over Business program applies a proven system for creating peak performance that will help you achieve success no matter what business you are in.

This book will give you the Mental Edge to overcome obstacles and take advantage of opportunity. The Mind Over Business approach is not a "rah-rah" motivational speech that promises the secret of success, gets you all pumped up and leaves you without the skills needed to succeed. It is, instead, a precise system that goes way beyond motivation to instill a lasting drive based upon individual values so you become unstoppable. People who are fearless, confident and competent in life are always the ones who find more doors open to them.

My system of breathing and relaxation techniques, goal setting and value linking, posture and mood, attitude and self-talk, visualizing success by design and creating performance anchors and cues is guaranteed to change your actions and improve your ultimate results. If you apply this program in its entirety, you will think clearly and precisely execute an action no matter what your goals are. Mind Over Business helps you avoid making rash decisions or responding emotionally to external situations.

Mind Over Business is one of the most valuable business books you will ever read because it applies your own lifetime of experience and knowledge to your personal pursuit of excellence. It will mobilize all your resources and teach you the right way to set and achieve any goal. This book takes business theory and sales training and makes it easy to use. *Mind Over Business* will show you how to get more out of every busy day as you become an expert at self-motivation and time management.

In addition to training business leaders, I work with the best athletes in the world, including men and women on several U.S. Olympic teams who have free access to the best trainers and best sports psychologists. But instead of having a psychologist that the U.S. Olympic team lets them use for free, many have searched me out and paid me because what I do works.

In the months leading up to the 2010 Winter Olympics in Vancouver, USA bobsled driver Steven Holcomb and teammate Steve Mesler hired me because they wanted something different and fresh. I worked with them on the dynamics of their team and guided them to understand and respect the potential restrictions, limits and strengths of their teammates, to stay in the moment, regardless of personal issues. As a result, the U.S. bobsled team took home the gold medal in its event, the four-man bobsleigh. (It also won its first World Bobsled Championship in more than sixty years during our time together.) And the team earned the much-coveted front cover of *Sports Illustrated*.

Now, following years of success in one-on-one and group consultations with top athletes and businesspeople, I've put these skills, exercises and concepts in a book from which anyone can benefit.

Athletes and businesspeople are similar, and at the same time, they are different. They are similar in that they have to be self-reliant: they have to go out on stage, perform and get the job done—alone. They are different in that the athlete uses his or her body primarily, while the businessperson uses the power of his or her brain and language. They both maintain an internal conversation, a self-supporting, positive pep talk that no one hears but them. And they have to perform. The bottom line is that if either—businessperson or athlete—doesn't perform, that person doesn't eat.

Great businesspeople are often confident and cocky, maybe downright arrogant. The same thing is true of great athletes—even if, outwardly, they know how to talk to the media, sounding level and at ease, totally humble and meek, they are not. Inside, they are prepared to tear your head off, find a way to win, and make sure that nobody will beat them. That's the way great businesspeople are, too.

Businesspeople look at selling, negotiating and value creation as a game. It's their Super Bowl, and they will make it happen; they will win. And instead of playing a Super Bowl once a year like the NFL, they're in their Super Bowl every single day.

Skater Sasha Cohen read my first book, *The Mental Edge*, and searched me out. She worked with me for about seven months before the 2006 Olympic Games in Turin, Italy.

She was a beautiful skater but one who lacked big event success. Physically, she was the best in the world, but mentally she was stuck. What I realized about Sasha right away was that she is an artist, which is what made her so amazing to watch. The sport of figure skating is naturally artistic, but at the Olympic level you need the perfect combination to excel. My job was to sharpen her mentally and give her the tools to blend her personality and athleticism to compete at the highest level. Once we established her goal, we went to work on making it a reality.

Her process was a long one because she was comfortable in her existing thought process—after all, it had made her a national star. She was known for being precise in what she wanted and was quick to change coaches or choreographers if she wasn't getting what her heart desired.

But she stayed with me right up to the Olympic competition, even calling me twice the night before her final skate in the long program. She had just skated an Olympic-best short program and was feeling the pressure. We talked at length, and I reminded her to do the same things she did during her almost-perfect short program. She came out on the ice for her long program and, as if in a state of shock, did not execute her performance cues. Her posture and facial expression alarmed me, which made me equally concerned about her breathing. To me—probably not to anyone else—she looked like a deer in the headlights, and she promptly fell on her first jump. The old Sasha would have cracked and all would be lost. The new Sasha bounced up and deployed her performance cue and finished strong enough to win the silver medal.

It Doesn't Matter Where You Start

My own success story is rather unusual.

I dropped out of high school in my senior year when my best friend committed suicide. I floundered for a time and finally got a GED when I was twenty-three. That was so I could get into the insurance business, because I didn't want to continue drifting from one stupid odd job that I hated to the next. From that point forward, I became successful, and I learned how to speak publicly and how to train seriously.

I soon became one of Prudential's top sales managers. I rose to the top 2 percent of all the company's sales managers in North America. Later, I moved to a smaller company and quickly became a vice president. But selling insurance and investments was not a passion of mine; I wanted to train athletes. I also wanted to be a professional speaker, and I made up my mind to do that, too.

At the ripe old age of twenty-seven, I started my own research center and a public speaking communications school, and it was a complete success and became a springboard for other successful ventures. Based on my past, there was no evidence I should ever have been able to do that. But *I made up my mind* that this was the track I was going to follow. Today I have a business and sports training center, BioDynamax Training Center in Capistrano Beach, California, where I train many of my clients.

I made up my mind to be an achiever, and I went out and developed the resources to meet my ambitions. My biggest obstacle was answering the recurring questions "What's your education?" and "Where's your degree from?" Today, there are students working on their master's theses and PhDs who are researching *my* work.

I've been an entrepreneur. I've experienced the highs and the lows; I've sold for a living. I've been in the trenches; I've made $250,000 a year selling a product that wasn't my own. I've earned my credibility, having built my business from scratch not once but twice.

Along the way, I've learned many hard lessons, but this one is paramount: You have to believe in yourself before you can sell yourself to somebody else.

Mind Over Business will help you reach your goals in business and in life. It grew out of my own heartbreaking personal experiences as the victim of a Ponzi scheme. I started over by applying the very practices and exercises that I taught others. I want people to see that the program in these pages has the power and ability to change a fixed mind-set.

Now is *always* the best time for a book that will improve your lot in life, whether the economy's good, bad or indifferent. It doesn't matter. No matter what your education, no matter what your background, there's a way to think and act that will allow you to maximize your potential. In *Mind Over Business*, I will share with you specific exercises that will change your way of thinking. Other books might have their value, but a lot of them ultimately let the reader down! They set readers up for failure because they don't address core issues, such as hard work and talent, strongly enough. The business world doesn't function that way.

I will teach you the skills you need to change your brain and impact your daily business activities in a logical, measurable manner. This book will help you build your own business success by giving you the tools you need to make up your mind and become undeniable. It doesn't matter what the goal or dream is. It doesn't matter whether you are self-employed, work for a large or small company or sell insurance or sandwiches.

Mind Over Business will teach you to use all of your apparent and even hidden talents in the best way possible and inspire you. The book is full of exercises that will change your life and business. These are the techniques I use with the world's best athletes and businesspeople, and now they are at your fingertips.

1

A Mental Edge for the Rest of Your Life

As the late, great philosopher Yoda said in a galaxy far, far away, "Do or do not. There is no try." "Doing" causes a result every single time. If you keep doing the same things, you'll get the same results—whether you like them or not. It's the law of life; it's the law of business.

When you follow the Mind Over Business steps and commit to the program, your chances of success will go up because you will be doing things differently. Don't pick and choose what you might want to try. Do all of it. If you do all of it, you are assured of earning a better result.

If you want to increase productivity on a manufacturing line, it's impossible unless you change something. Suppose you are a car builder. You can't just speed up one section of the assembly line without affecting the entire process. You must synchronize the entire system, man and machine, so there is harmony between all and so that peak performance can be achieved.

The aim of this chapter is to prepare your brain for the rewiring that will follow as you harmonize mind and body to take the actions needed for success. Over the years, it has become evident to me that every change of thought, every change in mental or emotional state, is followed by a shift in our physical state. A key component of Mind Over Business is learning to minimize your mind's distractions, counterproductive messages and signals to your body. It can work quickly, like it did for baseball pitcher Randy Johnson.

Randy was stuck with a negative message because of his team's lack of run production. The thought was "I must be perfect." He began to worry when he gave up a single run.

Johnson was already a superstar on his way to the Baseball Hall of Fame when I met him in Phoenix on May 8, 2001. Yet even he wasn't satisfied with his results, which were everything in his business. I met him by chance; we were both keynote speakers at a high-profile, all-day motivational program, killing time in the Green Room, waiting to be called on stage.

In Johnson's situation, it didn't matter how hard he tried. It didn't matter what he did last year or even yesterday. Results *now* were all that mattered in his job. He knew he was pressing his pitches and trying too hard because, as a team, the Arizona Diamondbacks were not scoring a lot of runs. He felt like it was his responsibility to carry the team until its run production increased.

We had a twenty-minute talk during which I asked him pointed questions about his process. He said, "I'm constantly in the position of trying to protect a small lead, or I'm afraid of making a mistake and giving up a run we can't match."

I said, "When you're throwing really well, what are you thinking?"

"I don't think then," Randy said. "I just throw."

"We've gotta get you back to that state," I told him. "It may be a reality that your team is not scoring runs. But what you're thinking is causing you to throw poorly. So let's change that. Suppose that your team is going to score enough runs. It's just as true to assume that; which assumption makes you a better pitcher?"

My direction to him was to become a "next ball pitcher."

"You can't control the hitter, your teammates in the field or your own batters," I said. "Assume the runs will be there and then forget about it. Put all your focus on that one next pitch and nothing else. You don't have to be perfect; just better your situation and throw mindless—you need to be mindful to go mindless—every time you pitch the baseball."

In other words, I told him to see the pitch called for by the catcher, feel the pitch go there, and let the sucker fly. I encouraged Randy to relax on the mound and trust himself. I also told him to believe his team would score the runs needed to win. This last result was out of his control, of course, but I believed his teammates needed to feel he was as confident in them as he was in himself. That's an important factor in team sports—and in team leaders, which Randy was.

I had Randy visualize on the mound what that next ball looked like, knowing he could block out everything but that next pitch. I had him see it, feel it, experience it, and then instructed him to go out and do it live against the Cincinnati Reds that very evening.

"Don't worry in advance or think 'What if . . . ,'" I said. "'What if' is only good if it's followed by a positive. Just throw the ball one pitch at a time."

That night, Johnson struck out twenty batters in nine innings to tie a major-league record. (He was already known as a great strikeout artist; he finished his career with 4,875 strikeouts, more than any other left-hander in history.)

The Diamondbacks were losing 1–0 in the fifth inning despite Johnson's personal heroics. They tied the game at 1–1 in the bottom of the sixth. It stayed 1–1 when Randy left the game after nine innings, denying him a victory for his Herculean effort. In the top of the eleventh, the Reds produced two runs, but the D-backs came back even bigger in the bottom of the frame with three runs and a thrilling, walk-off victory.

Randy Johnson's self-perceived problem of overpitching when his team was down or the game was close turned into one of the best nine innings of pitching in history, and he didn't even get the win! His team did, however, which was more important in the big picture, and he did everything in his power to get them there.

The biggest take-away from that story is the power of little things to do a lot. This standout moment in Randy Johnson's career happened because he realized the power of a single thought and how it could affect a performance. It was Mind Over Business to the max.

I love guys like Randy Johnson. They become superstars because they continue to grow beyond their first moment of broad success. They're a clear contrast with many mediocre athletes who are so prideful and full of themselves that they refuse to look at themselves honestly. They never maximize their potential because they are lazy or flat out don't care. It's the same in the business world. How is the person who learns but doesn't apply any better off than one who doesn't learn?

I will teach *you* how to condition your mind so that your body performs instinctively and unconsciously on a consistent basis. You will be guided by feelings of success and confidence that already exist in your mind and body and automatically trigger emotions, attitudes and actions that will make it possible for you to perform to your maximum potential.

Everyone has tremendous potential. Sometimes it's not as obvious as Randy Johnson's; maybe you're more like Cassie, who owns a small telemarketing firm. She felt she was maximizing her potential because she was working seventy to eighty hours a week. She realized, however, that she wasn't as successful as she could be and needed a complete overhaul, applying all the techniques that you'll find in this book.

Get with the Program! The Mind Over Business Program

If you want to scale Mount Everest, you don't just start climbing. You make sure you see the peak, and you learn exactly how high it is. You create a game plan and a personal fitness plan. Then and only then do you take the first step. This is a complete program that is best applied step by step the first time through. You can then pick and choose the skills that best fit your life and apply as needed.

In business a lot of people take the first step too soon because they don't know what they really want or how to get it. What you need is a complete set of mental and physical exercises—and a prioritized sequence for them—to prepare you for career and life performances that show you at your very best every day and in the most extraordinary of circumstances. See yourself on top of the real

Mount Everest—or your career's business equivalent—having enjoyed the rise to the top in a rewarding way and prepared to get back down safely. Then you can start your *real* life's climb.

What do you really want? Once you know that, imagine yourself in a business that is satisfying both financially and emotionally, and that gives you the ability to do what you want with your life. What would you look like really enjoying your business? What are some of the rewards for living this dream? Working on your own terms, perhaps? How do you interact with your family and friends? How do you spend your time? When you imagine that career being over and you look back over those work years and where they got you— was it worth it? If it was, by all means, take the first step.

This is the powerful concept of Finish Before You Start, which makes everyone more efficient. Your chance of success will rise dramatically if you perform this exercise. A related concept, Pre-Play, is the same principle but aligned with a smaller goal. For example, Pre-Play how you want your day to go. What are some of the things you can expect to happen throughout the day? See yourself handling those in the most efficient manner possible. What are some things that will tick you off or that have a tendency to ruin your day? How can you imagine heading them off at the pass and not letting them reach the point of aggravation? If that does happen, how can you change your attitude in advance to make sure you still control your day?

Every athlete I talk to, every team I train, every businessperson I work with, when I ask, "What do you want?" offers an answer that is some variation on "To be a big success." "Great," I say. "What's that going to look like? What's it going to feel like? Do you know what needs to be done? And what it's going to cost you? If you do, are you willing to pay the price? If you are, great, let's get it done!"

Now you are primed emotionally, as the brain is operating from a success mode and has a path to follow. But we live in a tough world, and there is a lot of competition out there. You can't just go out with a smiley face and conquer the world. You need to be in your Maximum Performance State (MPS) on a consistent basis. I describe it as being in the bottom of the ninth inning with two outs, bases loaded, the game on the line, and your team down by one run. In this electric situation, you want to be clearer and sharper than you have ever been in your life. In the business world, we need to be in this state every day. If you are running your own business, you can't come in to work and say, "Oh, it's just another Monday," and go through the motions. That's not going to work. You could be there till midnight and it's only the first day of the week. Why not maximize your performance? And you will when you get yourself into this state. A key component of MPS is the posture of a winner. You breathe like one, look like one, think like one, act like one. If you do it every single day, you will become a winner.

You need this kind of Consistent Resilient Action (CRA) to see you through. CRA is about making up your mind that you won't ever quit, you won't ever stop—you just *go*. You bounce back, you cushion the blows from daily life by your consistent, resilient action and understanding of the job at hand. You can make yourself this way with the tools found in this book. One of the most powerful things I've found in my life, again, is that people know I am not a quitter. Some think I am hardheaded—maybe even stupid. Fine! But I'm consistent and resilient. I never give up and I always give the task before me that something extra.

A primary building block in Mind Over Business is writing a Desire Statement. What do you really want? When you have a purpose-driven business and a corresponding mind-set, everything is easier and you become more efficient. The writing of your Desire Statement gives you purpose and a deep-seated drive. You are in the driver's seat; your desire is the focus, resulting in clarity in a chaotic world. Personally, I want a successful training center with multiple locations that will change people's lives, make me enough money so I can hire the right people and have some freedom. That's *my* desire. The reward is I can spend time with my kids, fly-fish or mountain climb. What about you? Do you want to be vice president of your company? Do you want to take care of your family in a more reliable way? Give your kids the college education they need to compete?

I'm going to show you how to write—and rewrite—a Desire Statement as well as a matching Reward Statement, first to establish what you want, then to state it as a goal. That will be followed by a Personal Action Plan, which is an inward and outward look at yourself—and how to get what you want in life.

The Personal Action Plan is not a business plan; it's a sketch of the skills and habits you already possess and the ones you need to acquire to be successful. If you are going to build a restaurant and plan to be the maître d' but you're not an outgoing, gregarious person, your Personal Action Plan will help you see that you might need to work on that.

Peak Performance is the notion of being on task 24/7/365. Every day is your Super Bowl. Every day is your World Cup. Every day you go to work, you are required and expected to perform well. Why not make peak performance a habit? If mediocre performance can be a habit, why not make peak performance your habit instead? When you see people that are true peak performers, they don't think about it, they just are.

When you go from "I want to" to "I will," to "I must," that's called Mindsetting. Your mind will be set; there will be no going back. It's cast in stone. It's not an exercise in futility; it's not a modest goal that you can easily accomplish. There is no reason to set your mind on something you know you can do. That's easy. "I'm not going to eat potato chips today." That's a goal, but you don't need to go through this big Mindsetting process for *that*. However, if you're going to buy a building and start a clothing exchange—or anything else you've never done before—you better make sure you have your mind made up that you are going to make that happen, or you're going to throw away a lot of money, time and effort with no return on investment at all.

Intertwined with Mindsetting is Value Linking, which gives you more reasons to set your mind on doing what it is you want to do. In the military, it's simple: the values are God, country and family. Or think about the Apollo 11 lunar landing. The United States made it a goal in 1961; the country reached its goal in 1969. It was a huge financial drain, but there was a major value link: superiority over the Russians. "Beat the Russians!" was our battle cry. That was a great example of linking a value to a task.

Speaking in terms of tasks, we live in a chaotic world that demands a great deal of us day in and day out. Every time we turn around, there is an earthquake, a tsunami, an economic crisis, people being murdered, political turmoil—you name it, we're dealing with it in some manner. It's a world that demands Clarity Amid Chaos, and that's something I can help you find.

On the job, businesses are being bought and sold, people are being hired and fired without explanation. At home, there are family challenges, babies screaming, teenagers proudly exhibiting anti-social tendencies, and parents and grandparents aging poorly. Chaos is all around us. How do we find clarity amid all that? By staying focused on the task at hand and realizing that we don't have control over the rest. Our reaction to it is what's important. To find Clarity Amid Chaos, you have to keep your mind sharp. You have to have that made-up mind to stay on task regardless of what goes on around you.

As you reassess the business world around you and its demands on you, I will help you design your life by the skillful use of Visualization exercises. You will see, smell, hear and taste the object of your desire. The more experience you can have with visualization, the more real what you visualize becomes, the stronger the signal to the brain and the better your chance of following through.

The internal dialogue that we all have is called self-talk; we are going to replace your normal, sometimes self-defeating self-talk with Performance Talk. Performance Talk is present tense and involves positive action toward a desired outcome. Most people never stop and think about what they say to themselves, they just say it. With the Mind Over Business program, you will pause and listen more carefully to how you talk to yourself and discover that when we talk to ourselves successfully, there is a different tone of voice, maybe even somebody else's voice—compared to when we dwell on failure, are miserable and unhappy or we don't believe in ourselves. Sometimes, it's subtle. Sometimes, it's just brutally obvious.

Positive experiences can be stacked to form anchors to success. A Performance Cue allows you to trigger those successes to change your body's posture, breathing and facial expressions, to set yourself in peak performance state. Performance cues happen all the time, often inadvertently, by habit. I will show you how to install them on purpose so that you can get yourself there whenever you need to.

The Instant Relaxation Technique (IRT) is something I developed to allow you to relax in an instant in the face of stressful situations in which you nonetheless have to perform. A relaxed mind is a sharp mind; you will acquire and apply this technique and create a Pavlovian conditioned response to relax on cue.

Throughout our lives, when we've done something successful, from tying our shoes to dressing ourselves, passing our first math test or attracting that first kiss, the action has created memories. A Success History Search is a conscious effort to replay past successes and see what your common threads are. They make you feel better immediately, and tying a cue to these memories will give those experiences more permanence.

Finally, all around us, there are Patterns of Excellence. Everything that we want to do, for the most part, has been done before. Are you willing to find out what the pattern is? Once you do—follow it. Too many people let their ego get in the way of success. They start a business and they think they can thrive just because they have a passion. But without a plan centered on a pattern of excellence, they will almost surely fail. Whether you want to sell cars, start an IT business or open a restaurant, there are patterns of excellence to be copied.

What to Expect

As you make up your mind to expand and maximize your potential, realize that *Mind Over Business* provides you with tools, not miracles. You may experience immediate success or you may notice a small cumulative effect that eventually snowballs into something significant. It will only take about six hours to read the book and do all the exercises. Commit to them for ten to fifteen minutes a day for twenty-one days; that's enough to change your life forever.

One of the things that will make this book more valuable to you than many other self-help or business development books is the way it shows you how to mobilize all your resources to maximize your potential. You must take action now. Now is the best time. Not tomorrow, today.

2

The Power of a Made-Up Mind

I was a visitor to a mental health hospital in Pueblo, Colorado, several years ago. And no, I was not a patient! During the visit, I was walking through the central grounds and a man ran past me as fast as he could with a big goofy smile on his face, yelling, "I am going to catch you, Wind!" He sprinted across the lawn, back and forth, repeating that line over and over as he went. He wasn't successful. He had enthusiasm, he had speed, he had drive, but he didn't have a clue that the wind exceeded his grasp.

Being successful in business demands the right attitude and the right actions. And if you don't have the right skill sets, you are doomed to failure. You will be chasing the wind.

I started a personal training gym for martial arts and athletes. But I had never taught martial arts before. To some people that made as much sense as a guy from Alabama starting a chain of Chinese restaurants. And maybe that's a fair criticism. But when I opened the gym, I talked to people who were already successful at it. One of my friends, who operates five very successful schools, said, "Ken, you need to become as good a student of business as you are of karate to make this thing work." That's what I did. While gyms all around me are failing, mine is doing better and better every month.

In this chapter you'll apply exercises that will teach you to make your thoughts precise to the task, that drive is better than motivation, and how to have Clarity Amid Chaos. Make up your mind to read all these and to do all the exercises.

Excuses or Opportunities: It's Your Choice!

A fifty-one-year-old corporate executive with a master's degree was stuck in neutral. He had started his career on the fast track. When new doors stopped opening for him a few years ago and were shown instead to younger men and women, he became embittered and blamed it on favoritism, nepotism, racism, ageism—every -ism but himselfism. "I show up on time and I get the job done," he said. *"It's not my fault!"*

A forty-two-year-old restaurant owner was struggling. She said, "It's the damn economy! We need a new president and then I will surely be all right. I only hope I can hang on that long!"

A twenty-four-year-old college graduate with a double major was ready to join the work force—only to find hundreds of people applying for the same good jobs. "I didn't go to school for this to happen," she said. "This is not fair!"

A thirty-one-year-old was making money hand over fist, only

to have the market change abruptly and potential new clients vanish from his radar. He cursed everyone, blamed the world and sank deep into debt, drinking heavily, hurting his family with his verbal barbs and defeatist attitude and eventually filing bankruptcy and walking away from everyone and everything. "My wife wanted all these things that put me in debt," he declared. "It's not my fault!"

A twenty-three-year-old with no sales or business experience earned a GED so he could enter the insurance and investment business. He did surprisingly well despite what most people perceived, from the outside, as his limitations. He became a top salesperson, making $250,000 a year in commissions. He left that industry to follow his dream of opening a sales training and business development school. This, in turn, fueled another passion: being a sports psychologist—even though he could hardly spell "psychologist" and had no formal training in the field. Through the calamity of a devastating car wreck and a colossal loss from a Ponzi scheme, he remained driven and passionate, telling his family and friends, "You can't always control what happens to you, but you can control your responses. Success is a choice, and I choose success. If it is to be, it's up to me!"

These five experiences were similar in that all these people had work-related challenges and setbacks. All had legitimate excuses for their situations.

There are millions of people like the first four examples, unable to enjoy the process of working, unable to put their education and life experiences to use, failing to understand the dynamics responsible for their situations. Number five was less educated than all the rest, had devastating setbacks, yet lived his dreams many times over, in all economic conditions.

Number five was *my* story.

It illustrates the power of a made-up mind. There is nothing more powerful than a made-up mind, especially in a difficult situation. Excuses, frustration and failure are everywhere. Happiness, contentment and true success are not.

For me, everything was working out as planned. Business was great, profits were high, with no business debt whatsoever—my operation was positioned nicely for a profitable sale with plenty of cash to try new ventures or retire. With more than a million dollars in personal assets and much more to come, no personal debt and the ability to walk away from my business at forty-three, life was good.

Just as soon as the plan peaked, it all came crumbling down, thanks to a few poor business decisions compounded by a failing national economy. Because it's one thing to set a plan and another to see it work perfectly.

This is my personal version of *Mind Over Business*. It informs everything I do with my clients, friends and family.

If It Is to Be, It's Up to Me

After everything in my life crumbled, I was alone with my goal and knew I was going to have to start over. This was the toughest part besides feeling like I'd let people down. I had to succeed; failure was not an option. I often worked through the night, thinking, writing, recording and doing paperwork, sometimes sleeping on the office couch at the gym. I was the janitor, bookkeeper, trainer, marketer, salesman, graphic designer, web developer—you get the idea. If it needed to be done, I had to do it.

I soldiered on alone against ever-mounting odds, no money, and no credit, just the power of a made-up mind. I adjusted my business plan, gave up thoughts of revenge and any hint of self-pity and "Why me?" and plowed full speed ahead.

I refocused on the things at which I excelled and committed to the building process with a totally positive attitude. Starting over was an exciting adventure and proof of the power of a made-up mind. An excruciatingly difficult setting provided a great opportunity to live what I believe in. I didn't know it at the time, but this disaster would soon make me much more money than I'd lost and help countless people from all types of businesses and walks of life along the way.

I was taken advantage of by friends who wanted my unwitting help to further a scheme that was disguised in plain sight as a legitimate business. It cost me once-valued friendships, family relationships, my life savings, my beloved home and my credit rating. Losing everything as a victim in a Ponzi scheme was a blessing and an education for me. It cleared the way for a better, more successful man to emerge. I created a six-point action plan that started with accepting responsibility for what happened.

First, I made up my mind that I would come back better than ever. I would take sole responsibility for what had happened. I checked my inventory of real and virtual assets and contemplated the best way to use what was left. I also made a decision to write this book after I came out the other side.

Second, I revisited past successes to create that passion and drive that fuels achievement.

Third, I decided to recommit my energies to Mental Edge training and guiding athletes via a new business, BioDynamax Training Center. Through it, I developed a new model and saw success before it happened.

Fourth, I wrote down my goals and an action plan based on my business model and resources.

Fifth, I began to use all the mental techniques in the Mind Over Business program to give me a real shot at success. I would not quit! It was not an option. I would not think about how hard it was or how unfair it was or complain about my difficulties. I focused, dove in headfirst and started swimming for my life with a smile on my face while sharks were trying to eat me alive. I controlled my self-talk, breathing, and posture, and this gave me a can-do attitude. Not some pop-psych masquerade, but a deep-seated drive that delivered consistent, resilient action. I visualized a new type of gym that became the BioDynamax Training Center—something never seen before, a special place for special people where the *Mind Over Business* techniques are writ large and in person.

Sixth, I further studied successful gyms and dojos and modeled their excellence. I didn't question or force myself to agree with them, I just *did*, I acted on what I observed. I decided to teach martial arts, although I had never done so, or even run a dojo. (I was a 2nd Dan [degree] black belt.) I found people who were highly successful and duplicated what I could. I patterned their excellence. The results exceeded all my expectations, as we had record months, month after month, right in the middle of a recession.

What worked for me can work for you, if you avail yourself of the exercises and make the commitment to the program.

You Can Do This

There are always opportunities. The American dream is dead in some people's minds, and in others', it's alive and well. If you decide to open a café, if you give it everything you can by studying successful cafés and dramatically taking the right actions based on what you observe, your chance of success will go up drastically. But if you think, "I'm going to give this a try and hope it works," you're doomed to failure.

A lot of people are afraid to commit to their dream or goal. They don't want to make a decision; they just vacillate back and forth, and then they never get anywhere.

The people who make up their minds say, "I'm going to do this; I'm not going to fail," and they're not afraid to fail. If it doesn't work out, they know they gave it everything they had, then they just lick their wounds and move on.

To illustrate this point, let me tell you about Jonathan. He started a gardening and tree trimming business, and he made up his mind to do it really well. He was successful to the point of making himself a millionaire. Emboldened by success in a field he knew so well, he decided on a whim to try opening a restaurant. Bad move! It ruined everything Jonathan had created in the gardening business. He lost it all because he tried to do something at which he wasn't skilled or reasonably prepared without following all of the other steps. He *tried*, but he didn't make up his mind based on all the other necessary factors: doing the requisite research, gaining experience, arranging financing, or patterning on a successful restaurant. Two years later, he was broke.

Just "trying" something rather than making up your mind and committing to it wholeheartedly undermines your ability to make a living and have a passionate belief in what you're doing. The people around you can tell the difference, from employees to family. The water-cooler chatter about your chances for success reflects what kind of person you are.

If you decide to open a flower cart and sell Dutch tulips, if you make up your mind you are going to do that and give it everything you can, and you take the right actions, studying flowers and successful flower carts, your chance of success goes up drastically. But selling Dutch tulips from a cart is a completely different business than selling roses in a store, and if you think, "I'm going to just give this a try and hope it works," you're doomed to failure.

Location Is Not Everything

Successful businesspeople grasp what is needed for success and don't waste time chasing the wind. They understand that business demands combining the right attitude with the right action. Anything less is, well, the following story:

A twenty-four-year-old man came to me for help. He and his father were starting a clothing line. He was so excited because this was going to be Pop's big break. His father, in his late forties, had already leased a retail space on Pacific Coast Highway in Laguna Beach, California, before they even had one stitch of clothing to sell.

I asked, "Why have a building before you have any clothes?"

"Because, as you know, Ken, location is everything."

Trying a different tack, I asked him about his game plan.

"We have this great logo and design and we are taking it to the street. It's our dream!"

As the conversation continued, it was painfully obvious they had no chance at success. They understood elements of a successful venture but not in an appropriate order of action and importance.

I asked, had his father ever worked for a successful clothing line before? The answer: *No*. Had he ever gone to design or business school? *No*. Had he ever sold clothing, worked with retailers or wholesalers? *No*. Did he have a mentor who was leading him through the process? *No*. Did he have unlimited funds so they could learn as they went? *No*.

They, too, were chasing the wind. Six months later they were out of business and out of money. They didn't understand the ways that success exceeded their grasp.

Successful People Have Drive

When you start up your car, you have potential power. When you put it in drive, the power is manifest and you move forward. The gas pedal supplies the motivation. Mash the gas pedal and off you will go—if the car is started and you are in drive. Put the car in park, however, and now step on the gas. What happens? Nothing but noise! The most successful people have the most drive and use motivation as needed.

I met Bob Bain through his son and daughter, whom I trained on the mental side to improve their volleyball skills. During my time with them, I got to know Bob and learn his story.

Bob was a skinny guy who grew up in northern Indiana. His brothers were all jocks, but he didn't have the build, so he decided to become a drummer instead. He moved to California in a rock band, playing 280 nights a year, eventually making his way to performing on a few TV shows. He realized the chance of big success was slim, but he was excited because the exposure on TV gave him an idea. He would start his own company—Bob Bain Productions! Talk about chasing the wind!

But Bob had a game plan. He went to the University of Southern California (USC) Law School, where he studied entertainment law. He told me that in his first two days of law school, he met more important, more interesting people than he had in years of playing in a band. That's when he was sure he wanted to be in entertainment, but not as a musician. It was all part of his grand plan to work on the industry's ground floor, to learn all that he could before embarking on his dream. He knew that the legal skills would be invaluable. That was part of his approach to success. It worked perfectly, and he had the drive to see it through. This otherwise average law student became president of the USC Entertainment Law Society in his second year.

After college, Bain spent fourteen years on someone else's payroll before he had garnered the skills, connections and belief that it was his time to shine. After toiling for a year in a traditional law firm, he took a meeting at MGM, and the interviewer liked him because he reminded her of her ambitious younger brother. At MGM (and later at Columbia) he worked in the business affairs departments, learned what a producer did, and decided, "That's for me." Also while at MGM, he played drums on the *Fame* tour with Janet Jackson when she was seventeen years old.

Columbia owned the rights to *The Monkees*, and Bob talked them into making him a co–executive producer of the 1987 sitcom remake. And while the series only lasted thirteen weeks, the experience was a great learning opportunity for him and led to a production job at Lorimar.

He produced a pilot for Fox in '89, and shortly thereafter, Fox hired him on a three-week trial basis in its business affairs/ production department. He stayed for seven years. That led to a position as vice president of special programming as he finally made his dream leap from administrative to creative. This was the final piece of the puzzle he needed to finally get out of the law—"It took me three years to get in and fourteen to get out!"

"I stayed through the tough times, endured and learned patience," Bob said. "It was the best graduate experience you could have. I met interesting people, did great deals, and made good money while crafting my career. Those experiences let me get to know everyone in the business and learn what I really loved."

Bob was patient. He put in the time, sought out and learned from people who had already arrived where he wanted to be, and waited for his right time to get there, too. I see Bob's awards shows all over television. In 2010 alone, Bob Bain Productions, Inc., was one of the most prolific music/event/variety/award producers in Hollywood, responsible for producing the Teen Choice Awards (Fox), the Kids' Choice Awards (Nickelodeon), the Mega Music Fest (Nickelodeon), the Billboard Latin Music Awards (Telemundo), the American Country Awards (Fox), New Year's Eve Live! (Fox) and the Critics' Choice Awards and Critics' Choice Red Carpet Show (VH1).

He is living his dream life and enjoying every minute of it. Not because he was lucky, not because he had some nonsensical motivation secret. Bob gained clarity with precise thought and ambition that kept him driving forward despite substantial obstacles. He knew *exactly* what he wanted to do and how to get there.

Find Clarity Amid Chaos

We live in a chaotic world. We are bombarded with messages of failure, doom and gloom. In 2010, the American airwaves and print media were full of recession, bailout and business failure woes as well as discontent between Democrats and Republicans, greenhouse gases, rising sea levels, and terrorism. The list of negatives went on and on. Why even try?

Yet, despite the naysayers, there is always opportunity for success.

If unemployment is 10 percent, that means 90 percent of all people are *working*.

If sea levels are rising, fix it, get a boat or forget about it.

What good does it do to worry in advance about a problem you can't control? One basic rule I started living by a long time ago was to remain clear amid chaos: "Don't worry in advance." Worry does no good and keeps you from precise thinking and right actions. There is always opportunity and there are always solutions to problems if you have drive and clear thinking.

I spoke at a business seminar at the Honda Center in Anaheim, California, where I was introduced by TV and radio sports personality Jim Rome, host of *The Jim Rome Show*. Rome is heard daily on two hundred radio stations and ESPN's *Rome Is Burning*. Before and after I went on stage, I had an opportunity to speak with him. Up until this time I never really thought much of him, good or bad. But after hearing his own success story, I had good reason to respect and admire his accomplishments.

Rome is a self-made phenomenon who was fortunate to discover precise thinking at a young age. When many of his peers were more focused on partying than school, he was carving out his career and making the sacrifices necessary to make his dream a reality. He understood that it would take more than education to be successful. It would take more than just believing. It would take clear thinking, the right attitude focused on the right actions, to develop the skill set he needed. He had to go against what was normal in his peer group and not be afraid to stand out in a crowd. He had the clarity of knowing what he wanted to do and did it—without worrying about what other people thought.

There Is Nothing More Powerful Than a Made-Up Mind

The beginning of precise thinking is making up your mind.

Bob Bain didn't *hope* he would one day operate a television production company. He made up his mind!

Jim Rome didn't *wish* to be a broadcast sports personality. He made up his mind!

I didn't *try* opening a training center. I made up my mind!

We all made up our minds and made sure we had the right attitude and actions for success. We filled in the gaps of what was missing and gathered the needed skill sets for success. This can become a problem for many as they get so caught up in acquiring skills. They become perpetual students, never confident they know enough to become masters.

On the other hand, many unqualified people embark on careers or business doomed to fail because they began purely on emotion. You can find people at the far ends of the spectrum that have had success, but most all of them knowingly or unknowingly followed the concepts behind *Mind Over Business*.

Warren Buffett didn't get lucky. He educated himself, calculated his risks and had the drive to see his desires through.

When Lawrence K. "Larry" Dodge founded American Sterling Insurance in 1977, he didn't just give it the old college try. He made up his mind to build a tremendous insurance company from scratch and embraced the precise thinking to see clearly what needed to be done. At twenty-seven years of age he acquired a national insurance group, making him the youngest CEO of such a company, a benchmark that still exists to this day. In 1971, he acquired a controlling interest in a national bank and became the youngest national bank chairman, another benchmark that still survives. Today he is the founding chairman, CEO, director and majority stockholder of American Sterling Corporation and its subsidiaries.

On a different scale, Ben Clymer made up his mind to have his own body shop and acquired the skill set needed to be successful. He labored and managed at other shops until he had the tools to succeed and start his first company in 1972. Today he is a Southern California brand name, operating as Ben Clymer's Body Shop. His goal was to establish a business known as much for its dedication to customer service as for its craftsmanship. A man with incredible drive, he operates in Riverside, Yucaipa, and Moreno Valley, California.

It Starts with a Vision

All of the success stories you just read share several common threads. They all:

- Started with a vision of what they dreamed of achieving
- Acquired the needed skill set for their particular vision
- Made up their minds to go for it 100 percent—not just try once and abandon ship short of land
- Insulated themselves from the chaos and negative thinkers around them by minimizing contact with negative media and people

Their precise thinking allowed them to go against the grain and do what needed to be done whether they wanted to or not. They are all a lot like you with their own individual strengths and weaknesses. If *they* can do it, so can *you*. You may not have the capacity, opportunities or even desire to be the next Warren Buffett, but how about becoming a really good investment advisor? What about opening the interior design business you have daydreamed about?

What's *your* vision? What do you dream of doing? How do you want to spend a good part of your life? What do you *really* want?

When you set goals this way, you have a better chance of success. And once you set the goal, look at how you can overcome the inevitable obstacles. What are the personal dilemmas you will encounter?

I will teach you how to become more assertive with yourself. Visualize. See it, feel it—experience reaching your goal. There are all kinds of books on how to run a business. There are all kinds of books on how to close a sale. There are all kinds of books on how to give a speech. But how do you get yourself conditioned mentally to be able to do those things? That's what this book's about.

A lot of people think that you're either born into success or you're not. If they think they themselves weren't so lucky, game over. But when you look at successful men and women around the world, you'll see that there are similarities among them and one of the most consistent is the presence of precise thought. They knew what they wanted to do and how they wanted to do it, and they found a way to make it happen. It wasn't an accident, and they didn't win the lottery.

Everyone is average at most things, but each of us has something at which we can usually excel over others. That's going to be true for people who are successful. With that, you wouldn't call them motivated people, you would call them *driven* people. They are driven to make a concrete casting business work. They are driven to make their automotive body shop work. And drive is always better than motivation, because motivation is the fuel in the car. Drive is the engine. If you have both, now you have incredible power.

Charlie wasn't a particularly motivated guy. He didn't go through his days positive and pumped up. The guy just went to work at his salvage yard every day an hour earlier than everybody else and did everything that needed to be done, whether he wanted to or not.

"I would never ask my employees to do something I wouldn't do," he said. "I was the first one there in the morning and the last to leave at night."

He built a successful business and eventually retired from it at fifty-two years old.

Charlie started with the power of a made-up mind. You make up your mind that you are going to do something, you are going to put aside being wishy-washy, you are going to put aside not knowing what your thing is, and then it follows that once you decide what you are going to do, you've got to have a plan, you've got to have the right ingredients every day, and you apply them in the right order. You can expand your success by adding other ingredients or other steps, but your initial success is the result of starting on the right track and repeating the same behaviors, keep doing again and again what you've been doing.

Along the way, you pattern the excellence of others, like Charlie did. He didn't just decide he was going to open a junkyard; first he went to work for a thriving junkyard. He had a friend who was already in the business who groomed him. From a young age, Charlie—a onetime juvenile delinquent who went on to be a U.S. Marine with two tours of Vietnam in his portfolio—learned all he could about the junkyard business. He had to learn how to buy, how to sell, how to price things, how to hold on to inventory, and how to do the requisite paperwork. There is a tremendous amount of salesmanship in the salvage business—that was news to me!—and Charlie had to develop that as a skill set, too. Most of us would just take that for granted. It's salvage. You go and you strip cars, you pile up the parts—Ford here, Hyundai there—and the customers hunt for them. But it's more complicated than that.

Charlie sold parts to auto repair places. He sold to small car dealerships. He sold parts to hot rod enthusiasts. How much can you get for one carburetor over another? What makes this one worth $80 and that one $120? He also had to know people. Of course, everybody wants a discount; everybody wants to walk in the door and be considered a "special" customer. So salesmanship was a huge part of Charlie's success.

Charlie eventually owned and operated multiple salvage yards, patterning his business on that of his friend's, making improvements that worked well for him—and grew an operation so successful that he retired young.

Imagine a Lifetime of Clarity

I'm often asked, "If I have a cluttered mind, can I change that? If my thinking is kind of like my desk and it's always covered with stuff, can I actually come out of that fog?"

The answer: Absolutely!

Make up your mind to what you really want, link your values and your true desires together, and then you will get more focused. You will be able to contemplate, meditate and have Clarity Amid

Chaos—which is a personal challenge for me, because so much in life excites me. You must have a central focus, a beacon that leads you out of the darkness.

What is your central purpose in life or business? That must become your focal point. If things in your life don't support that, cut them out. If I'm writing ten books at the same time, where is my clarity going to be? I must tell myself, "I'm going to make *this* book priority number one." The other nine go on the back burner, and I won't move on to the next one until the first is complete.

Living your dream isn't easy, and it requires sacrifice. Are the sacrifices worth it? To a lot of people, they're not. They can't just pick up and leave their family, they can't just change careers in midstream because of a whim.

At the same time, you have one life to live. Maximize your dreams, maximize your potential—find the balance. The sooner you can follow your dream, the less encumbered you will be. Crazy people do outstanding things that we look at and admire. Somebody had to be the first to climb Mount Everest. Whoever is first at something is typically a lunatic, and then all of a sudden that person succeeds through the power of a made-up mind and becomes a hero that others respect and admire. Other people think, "Oh, if that person can do it, *I* can do it."

3

What Do You Really Want?

Some people take a job because it is there—the low-hanging fruit.

They go to a school because it let them in.

They study a major because it was easy or because Dad did it.

They often lack a clear, precise purpose in life or business. They don't know what they want; they just hope for something good. If they do set a goal, and they don't get it, they consider themselves a failure.

If you shoot for the moon and you don't make it, you land among the stars. Often, a large goal missed is more valuable than a small goal made. If you made $500,000 last year and set your goal to make $1,000,000 this year, and you actually finished with $700,000, is that so bad? If your goal is to make $50,000 this year, and you make $47,000, is that failure, or is that success? If your income the previous year was $30,000, it's all in the perspective or the starting place.

That's successful. That $50,000 goal pushed you harder to get there, and that's the power of goal setting.

Hugh McCutcheon, head coach for the USA Men's National Volleyball team, hesitated when I said that the first thing I wanted him to do was set his goal as a gold medal.

His response was "We can't set that as the goal yet; we don't know if we're good enough."

"Hugh," I said, "if you want to be good enough, you need to set that as a goal. You need to go for it, and then peel backward to 'What do we need to do to get there?'"

He wasn't comfortable with that at first, and then after our second or third session together, he did set the goal as a gold medal. Then we focused on the steps that it would take to get there, such as being in the top ten at the team's next tournament, qualifying for the Olympics and, ultimately, looking at the gold medal around each teammate's neck. That was the endgame.

I convinced Hugh that we could better his team's chance of success by setting this goal. That's all we can do, because there are no guarantees in business, sports or life.

There are two basic types of goals: attaining the best and attaining your best. When you're on the volleyball team, there's only one gold medal. But if you're in sales, for instance, you can set a goal to hit $100,000—a lot of people do that, and there is no reason you can't reach that goal. There may be only one top salesperson within your company, but that doesn't mean you can't make a really good living and be a winner at being number two—or even number six.

Hugh was a great coach and outcoached the world. When you have that one goal of the gold medal, and everybody else from all these other countries is trying to do that, too, it still comes down to this: the ones that don't succeed probably didn't have a clear-cut goal, and they didn't have a clear-cut action plan. And some just don't have the talent. You have to have both, and then your chance of success goes up in direct proportion to taking the proper steps along the path.

Dream Big, Work Hard

Desire is more important than reality when it comes to achieving your dreams. The more desire you have, the bigger the internal fire. Things that were once unrealistic or a dream are now attainable. This is not the same as wishing or hoping. Desire is what makes you rise early, stay up late, and do what needs to be done whether you like the hours or not.

In business, like sports, it's not always the most talented person who wins. It's the one who wants it the most, the one who will out-work and outsmart the opposition and who refuses to see failure as anything but feedback.

In this chapter, I will teach you how to craft a Desire Statement that will clarify what you really want in life. This will be a vital block in making you relentless in the pursuit of building to your goal.

Your Desire Statement starts with a simple "I want to" instead of "What's realistic for me?" (We will get real a little later.)

It might start rather vague: "I want to have my own business" or slightly more precise: "I want to be a professional photographer" or very precise: "I want to be an action sports photographer."

You can have Desire Statements for skill development: "I want to be a better public speaker," "I want to better manage my time," or "I want to close business at a higher ratio."

Regardless of your desire when you create the statement, putting it on paper starts the process of moving it from a dream to a reality. The act of writing shows you are ready for a commitment at some level.

Emmitt Smith, the great Florida Gator and Dallas Cowboy running back (as well as the NFL's all-time leading rusher) was told by his high school coach, "It's a dream until you write it down." Emmitt followed his coach's advice, frequently writing down his most fervent desires and revising them as he went along. His first was not to be the NFL all-time leading rusher; that came later. In 1993, after being in the NFL for just three years, he wrote down that he would break Walter Payton's all-time rushing record, and on October 27, 2002, despite being thought of as too slow and too small, he did it! (By the way, if you don't know Emmitt Smith from football, maybe you would recognize him as a winner of ABC's celebrity competition *Dancing with the Stars*.)

You might reasonably ask, "How does writing down a desire translate into achieving a goal?"

When you write, you create a clear mental picture—involving more senses and brain activity—of yourself accomplishing a task, running the football a certain way, closing at a higher ratio or being an action sports photographer. You are creating a connection between your conscious mind and your body, providing a blueprint that allows you to believe these things are possible and to pursue them. Writing shows commitment—the act of writing helps clarify the goal by involving more senses. This connection activates a subconscious process that begins working automatically to improve your performance and moves you closer to your goal. It creates opportunities to take you beyond your prior, self-imposed limits. Obstacles that might once have seemed too huge to overcome become negotiable hurdles that we are able to go over, through or around.

When you create your Desire Statement, don't hesitate to think big!

Big desires cause the brain to think big and learn new skills quickly. TV producer Bob Bain told me that he went from being an average student to an excellent one, entirely because of his Desire Statement. That's not surprising, because your mind tends to move toward dominant thoughts, and if your Desire Statement is strong and compelling, you will activate that part of the brain to move beyond normal thinking and trigger subtle physiological activity that can help turn a desire into reality.

In working with businesspeople and athletes at all levels, I've found that weak desires set weak fires; in other words, there is not enough fuel to burn—so they wear out easily—and good things don't happen. I hear things like "I *wish* I could sell better" or "I am going to *try* and be more assertive" or "If things work out, it would be cool to be a pro athlete." But once they think through those desires a little more clearly, define them better and write them down, most people immediately feel that those same vague "iffy" goals are now tangible and attainable.

Many years ago, I gave a "Mental Edge for Sports" seminar at a Holiday Inn in Laguna Niguel, California. Since it was close to home, my then ten-year-old son, Bryce, went with me and handed out seminar guides to the attendees. When everyone was seated, the seminar began.

As I began speaking, I looked out in the audience and there was my ten-year-old, taking notes in his own seminar guide. I was teaching the section on the value of writing it down and using Desire Statements as a key in goal setting.

At ten years of age Bryce wrote down, "Someday I will play volleyball at the Pyramid." The Pyramid was a new, very cool gym where the Long Beach State University 49ers, a perennial top five college volleyball team, played. Just the wild-haired dream of a ten-year-old—or so it seemed. After all, he hadn't even played indoor volleyball at that point in his life.

Bryce started playing club volleyball at twelve, didn't play at thirteen, played again at fourteen but rarely saw the court. At fifteen he started to figure the game out a little, and at sixteen he was a setter for a team that won a silver medal in the Junior Olympics.

At seventeen, he played half a club season and at eighteen didn't play club at all. He played high school volleyball in a solid program, but when the Long Beach State University 49ers coach didn't come knocking with a scholarship, Bryce went to our local junior college, Irvine Valley College, and excelled under the coaching of Tom Pestolasi. He led the team to a league championship and to the semifinals of the state championship, making all-league and winning numerous team awards. But still no interest from Long Beach State.

Bryce, after all, was barely six feet and weighed 160 pounds, and Long Beach State was a major Division 1 college powerhouse. My son thought of giving the game up or going to play in the Midwest or at an East Coast school, but one day, unbeknownst to us, the Long Beach team's all-American setter got injured and the coach needed an emergency backup. The Long Beach coach reached out to the Irvine Valley coach, and he recommended Bryce. Out of the blue, Bryce got a call from Long Beach State head coach Alan Knipe saying, "We want you to come play for us!" *Wow!* Neither one of us could believe it.

My mind drifted back to the day almost a decade earlier when that ten-year-old boy wrote down his dream in a seminar notebook. Some may say, "That's just a coincidence." I say coincidence becomes reality when you put yourself in line for something to happen. And Desire Statements cause a surprisingly high number of coincidences.

Your Plan Starts Here

Here's what it comes down to: you are going to work forty to sixty hours a week anyway, right? Why not maximize your potential? Why not get excited about it? Why not take that same time commitment that you have to put in anyway and get something more out of it by focusing on the reward instead of doing it with a 78 percent effectiveness rate?

When you think about it that way, the most interesting thing happens. Your time goes by faster. If you want to make a job really drag, give it half effort. If you want a job to just blow by, give it everything you've got. It's amazing how that happens.

When you put your mind to an activity or a goal, you start attracting people, things and circumstances into your life that make that happen. You become more aware and attuned to opportunity. You are then reading and focusing differently. There is nothing magical here. There is nothing mystical here. The law of attraction simply puts you in a position mentally to become aware of your surroundings and how they relate to your goal. And there is overwhelming evidence that when you have a Desire Statement and you have the passion toward it that a Reward Statement gives you, the law of attraction will start working in your favor.

If your Desire Statement is important enough for you to make a strong commitment to it—that is, for you to decide that you will do whatever it takes to make it come true—it will become a powerful motivator that allows you to pursue your goals aggressively. This will take you beyond typical goal setting to Mindsetting. And as I will keep telling you, there is *nothing* more powerful than a made-up mind.

There are seven steps to creating a compelling goal, one that will cause a burning desire and the mind-set to make it happen. They are:

1. **Desire Statement.** Write down what you really want—your deepest desire for business success.
2. **Reward Statement.** Write down what you'll get for achieving your desire.
3. **Personal Action Plan.** A plan for self-management and giving yourself the proper path to follow. This is an action plan based on success strategies of people who have done it before.
4. **Belief.** Consider whether you really believe that you possess the ability and all the pieces necessary to be successful. If you don't, there's no reason to set the goal, right? These steps all logically lead one to the next.
5. **Pay the Price.** Consider whether you're willing to pay the price. Are you willing to do the things that need to be done whether you want to or not?
6. **Value Linking.** Link the most important things in your life to your desire or your quest. They will give you added power and resolve when the going gets tough.

7. **Set the Mind.** Now the mind is set. The desire is now a goal, "I will be CEO of General Electric by the time I'm fifty." It's now more powerful than a desire.

DESIRE STATEMENT

First, write a Desire Statement of your own. Spell out as many of your business desires as you like. You may certainly have more than one! The act of writing them out and comparing them will allow you to focus on the most important. Just let them come to mind freely and write them down. List in hand, go through and identify which one is the most important to you *right now*. Make it as simple or detailed as you like.

The most important thing is this: *Get started!* You can make adjustments later.

Your Desire Statement might look like this: "I want to be our company's next regional vice president."

Or it might be more detailed, like this: "I want to be our company's next regional vice president, establish new sales records for my region, make $200,000 a year and have a motivated, self-driven sales force."

Maybe yours will be like one of these two: "I want to have my own fishing guide service," or "I want to have my own fishing guide service in Southern Colorado from May to October with a focus on teaching fly-fishing."

I believe that precise thought on goals and actions will attract the people, circumstances and opportunities necessary for success. To succeed, your Desire Statement must be motivating *to you*, and as you read it and write it over and over, it should turn your desire into a burning passion. Do you think it was realistic for Oprah

Winfrey to ever think she would one day be a one-name, billion-dollar brand known around the world as just "Oprah"? Or that she would own a television network with her name on it?

It's time for *you* to write the first draft of your Desire Statement. Dream a little and stretch yourself here:

_____

_____

_____

I can't say it enough: There is *nothing* more powerful than a made-up mind. If you commit yourself to the Desire Statement you wrote above, you will move toward this dominant thought. Rewrite your Desire Statement every morning and every night for the next seven days. During the course of the exercises in this book, your statement will be rewritten and will evolve from desire ("I want to") to goal ("I will").

Even if it doesn't change and you already know what it says, putting it down on paper again and again will help reinforce it. Read it each time with enthusiasm and belief. This will keep the desire at the forefront of your conscious mind.

It is also okay to modify the statement as you respond to feedback. Feel free to let it grow and take on new meaning, becoming ever more real.

REWARD STATEMENT

When you focus on the value you receive as the fulfillment of your desire, it, in turn, creates more desire. It adds fuel to the fire. Your consistent thoughts of a coveted reward will increase your motivation and make your Desire Statement come true.

Consider this Desire Statement: "I want to be our company's next regional vice president, establish new sales records for my region, make $200,000 a year and have a motivated, self-driven sales force." Its corresponding Reward Statement might be: "So I can see my kids go off to the colleges of their dreams while enjoying my house and pool and NBA Basketball season tickets and have the money to retire in comfort while enjoying world travel."

A Reward Statement should be unique to you. What will you get from your achievements, both tangible and intangible? List all the rewards you can. Then, when things get tough, remind yourself what this is all about, and your focus will go back to your intended reward instead of the drudgery of another airport and hotel, encountering another stubborn, unresponsive salesperson or the boss that just cut your support staff.

Rewrite your Desire Statement here and then follow it with your first Reward Statement:

DESIRE STATEMENT

_____

_____

REWARD STATEMENT

_____

_____

These are the first steps in turning wants or dreams into reality. By doing this exercise you are clarifying what you really want and giving your mind a path to follow. You will be motivated to quickly acquire the skills needed for success and start attracting the people and circumstances to make your dream a reality.

PERSONAL ACTION PLAN

Now that you have created Desire and Reward Statements, we can move on to your Personal Action Plan. This is what it takes to make success happen. Without it you are like a ship full of precious cargo speeding out to sea without a directional rudder; keep on that ignominious path and it won't be long before you're another forgotten shipwreck at the bottom of the deep blue sea.

A Personal Action Plan takes inventory of your assets and liabilities and then works hard to minimize your liabilities and maximize your assets. For instance, you have an education from UCLA. That's an asset. How do you maximize that? Your liability is you have a speech impediment. How do you limit the risks from that? Do you worry on the liability too much, making it worse?

Naismith Memorial Basketball Hall of Famer Bill Walton had a terrible speech impediment while a student at UCLA—although it didn't stop him from being named College Player of the Year for three straight seasons. I remember hearing him in an interview and being embarrassed for him. You could hardly understand the poor kid.

In the NBA, few players could challenge the dominance of the six-foot-eleven center. His résumé in the league includes being an NBA champion (1977, 1986); NBA Finals MVP (1977); NBA MVP (1978); playing on the All-NBA First Team (1978), the NBA

All-Defensive Team (1977, 1978) and the NBA All-Star Team (1977, 1978); election to the Naismith Memorial Basketball Hall of Fame (1993); and being named "One of 50 Greatest Players in NBA History" (1996).

Incredibly, when his NBA career neared an end, he set a goal to be a sports announcer. Give me a break! The guy could barely speak!

But Bill made up his mind that in his second career, he could make a living with his mouth, not his body. And he did it! A long-time friend, I asked Bill for some more details on how he set a seemingly impossible goal—and achieved it. Here's what he wrote back to me:

> I was a very shy and reserved young man who could not speak at all without severely stuttering until I was twenty-eight years old. Always a success in the classroom and on the basketball court, I took refuge in the things that I did well as a youngster. Being a straight A student and having athletic abilities covered the deficiencies that limited my overall growth and development. The game of basketball was my religion, the gym my church. It was a convenient way of avoiding my responsibilities of developing my human relation skills.
>
> When I was twenty-eight, a chance encounter at a social event with Hall of Fame broadcaster Marty Glickman completely changed my life. That day, in a very brief, private conversation (one way, mind you, since I literally could not speak at the time), Marty explained, patiently and concisely, that talking, communicating, was a skill not a gift or a birthright and that like any skill, whether it be sports, music, business or whatever, it needed to be developed over a lifetime of hard work, discipline, organization and practice. Marty gave me some simple tips that day

and then encouraged me to take those keys and apply them to methods of learning that I had received from the special teachers that I had come across in my life, particularly the six Hall of Fame basketball coaches that I had played for throughout my career. The beginning of my whole new life was as simple as that.

No gimmicks, tricks or shortcuts. Just the realization that, with some help, guidance and a lot of hard work, I, too, could do what seemed so easy, simple and natural to everyone else, yet seemed impossibly out of my reach and comprehension.

What Marty gave to me—the gifts of how to learn, of how to practice—has changed my life and given me a whole new life. I have gone from a person who literally could not say 'Thank you,' to someone who makes his living as a television commentator and public speaker. I have also become a spokesperson for the National Stuttering Foundation.

The tips that Marty Glickman gave me almost twenty years ago that I still use and apply every single day are, in no particular order:

- Slow down your thoughts—think about what you are saying now, not three or four sentences ahead. Don't be in a hurry.
- Communicate not with speed, but rather with concise, analytical content.
- Chew sugarless gum to strengthen the muscles in your jaw and to get your mouth/jaw moving.
- Read out loud—it doesn't matter what the subject is, just do it . . . a lot.
- When you are comfortable reading out loud, move in front of the mirror and watch yourself, as others will see you speaking.

- Identify the sounds that cause you the most trouble—for me they are D's, H's, S's, Th's and W's (on some days I can't say a single one)—find written material that contains a lot of these sounds and go back to the start of this list and start over.
- Become a teacher—to anyone, anywhere, on any subject—start with young children and a topic that you know—they won't care about your limitations—all they care about is that you are willing to spend time with them and are trying to give them the gift of knowledge.
- Move forward and don't be afraid to fail—confidence will come from repetition—if I can do it, why can't you?
- When you stumble—stop, then start again—find your pace, your rhythm, your game—everyone makes mistakes—it's what you do after those mistakes that will determine your ultimate success and happiness—they mean you're a player.

"That's it," Bill concluded. "For me, no magic, no medication, no gimmicks, no shortcuts, no tricks . . . Just a plan, a vision, and a dream that maybe, someday . . . Learning to speak was my greatest accomplishment in life and I work on it every day."

Many years and a lot of hard work later, Bill is a respected network basketball analyst. He has won a number of Emmy Awards, and in 2009, the American Sportscasters Association named him one of the top fifty sportscasters of all time. (There is even a Facebook fan page devoted to him called "Bill Walton Is the Best Announcer Ever.")

Look at the reality of your current situation. What do you need to do or acquire to make success happen? Now is the time to take stock of your talent, skills and situation and take action to fill in the gaps.

A Personal Action Plan is different from a business plan. Many business plans end up being nothing more than exercises in futility because the writer doesn't understand the most important thing: the ability to take the massive personal action and responsibility necessary to acquire what is needed to be successful—whether those in the business want to or not.

Writing a business plan is easy: just buy a software template program and fill in the blanks; research the market, add a fabricated mission statement and look at the plan, sitting on the shelf, with pride. Investors desire them. Banks insist upon them. Consultants manufacture them. And once you write one, success is imminent, right? Wrong! The most important key to success is a Personal Action Plan. Your chance of success triples when you put yourself on the right course.

I have trained some of the world's best athletes and I see a common thread: they always have a Personal Action Plan. Kobe Bryant improves every off-season because he commits to acquiring a new skill. Three-time Olympic gold medalist in volleyball Karch Kiraly constantly tweaked his training and skill development with a precise Personal Action Plan.

Denise, a young investment advisor I once trained, had a problem with what she called "stinkin' thinkin'," and even though she worked for a great boss and a great company, she was failing. She wanted to be in the business but didn't like the selling part.

Denise came to one of my seminars, and she liked what she heard. She immediately took the concept of self-talk (Chapter 5) from that seminar and applied it to the way she viewed her business. She learned that how she talked to herself could have a huge impact on her results, and so she began having quiet, internal conversations with herself in the most positive way. What she did for a living was something she was already passionate about. How we talk to ourselves has a huge impact on our actions and our attitudes toward our actions. Denise realized this, changed her attitude, changed how she talked to herself, and it gave her a better overall attitude. She then attended one of my training programs to learn how to communicate better and to work more on the mental side of selling. Today she is one of the top salespeople in her company, loves the job and has all the time in the world to spend with her family and live a really good life.

After she wrote her Desire Statement and contemplated all the rewards of this achievement, I had her list all the reasons why she could be successful. She thought about her company, how it was rated, its excellent training program and the total respect she had for her regional manager. The boss was ethical, honest and made a ton of money. He liked helping people with insurance. He thought he was doing a good thing.

Denise considered the income potential of selling financial services for a living. Where else can a high school graduate make six figures in a professional world? She thought she was a natural for the business, because people liked dealing with her. She was a nice, gregarious woman with a big smile that people found attractive.

But she had her limits.

Denise lacked confidence that she could sell effectively. Selling was not in her family history. It was a dirty word with many of her friends and relatives. She found it difficult to do things like cold-calling and networking with her friends to earn their business. She did not want to be like the stereotypical, annoying insurance agent, pitching policies to everybody she knew, but that's the model for most sales jobs to start. She wasn't an aggressive person in that mold. People liked her because she was laid back and mellow and nice.

She turned around these liabilities by being honest with herself, identifying her weaknesses and committing to working on herself. She listed her strengths for success alongside her limitations to success, eventually creating her Desire Statement.

DENISE'S STRENGTHS

- A solid company, well respected
- Great training program
- Great leadership
- I like my job and the freedom and control I have over my workday
- Great income potential
- People like me.

DENISE'S LIMITATIONS

- Lack of confidence
- I don't really like selling
- I wish it was easier
- I'm not aggressive

DENISE'S DESIRE STATEMENT

I will be a successful insurance agent with a six-figure income that allows me to live comfortably. I will be a leader in my company and enjoy the process of selling.

Together, we examined her Desire Statement, and it was clear she really *wanted* to be successful. It was also obvious that she was conflicted. She needed clarity or there could be no commitment. I asked her, "Could you get this potential with any other job?"

"No," she said, which made her realize she was ready to change.

I asked her, "Are you willing to acquire what is needed?"

Denise said, *"Yes."*

"Are you willing to pay the price of success?"

"Yes."

She then wrote her first Personal Action Plan. This is what she wrote:

I will become more confident and aggressive and learn the science of selling, which will make selling easier.

I challenged her with one word: "How?"

She thought a moment and picked up on one of the seminar's suggestions:

I will read a book a week for twelve weeks and listen to an audio development program once a week for twelve weeks. I will also enroll in self-development classes.

The real challenge for Denise? She hated to read!

I gave her two books and told her, "How quickly and thoroughly you read these books is a direct reflection of your commitment to success." She read them both in two days. She then enrolled in my Mental Edge training program, showing up on time and staying late for every class. Within one week she was selling more, and at the end of the first month she had doubled her best month's production. After twelve weeks, she was a completely different person. *This* is what a Personal Action Plan will do for you, too.

In your Personal Action Plan, first identify your strengths and limitations and write them down. (Strengths are always easier than facing up to limitations, but you'll be a smarter person for acknowledging both.)

Analyze these areas for concern:

- Is my thinking helping or hindering me?
- What skills or knowledge do I need to acquire?
- Do I eat to maximize my potential (it's amazing how much food affects performance)?
- Am I maximizing everything I have, including my business and/or personal resources?
- What are the three most important things I need to act on immediately?

Based on your answers to these questions, you can create a detailed action plan for yourself that highlights the most important things you need for success:

- How many hours a day will you study?
- What is your goal for each day?
- Will you seek outside coaching?
- How will you adjust your diet to have lasting energy and be sharp all day?

Figure out how you can share your strengths with as many people as possible. That's your personal inventory, your warehouse full of products. Your product is worthless if it's sitting in the warehouse. Your strengths are worthless if nobody knows about them, so you have to find a way to get them out there.

Your limitations—do they matter? Can you keep them? Can you

hide them? Or do you need to get rid of them? Some people spend time on their limitations when they shouldn't. For instance, we often see creative types who lack organization think they're compensating by putting more energy into getting organized. In the end, however, it hinders their creativity. What makes them money? Creativity, not organization. You need enough organization to be functional and not trip yourself up. They might do better to hire somebody who can keep them more organized. At the same time, a person who is analytical and precise may not need to spend time on creativity. That's not valuable to them.

People waste a lot of time and energy working on things they don't need. You know what your job requires, what your dream requires. If you are going to be a mountaineer, don't spend a lot of time on indoor rock climbing. They are different sports. Don't bring a football to a basketball game. Don't bring a knife to a gunfight.

MY STRENGTHS

MY LIMITATIONS

_____

_____

_____

_____

Now that you have your personal inventory, it's time to decide on how to use it wisely. Take a look at your desires. What do you currently possess that will help make them real? What's an apparent liability that gets in your way? Do more of what you do well; do less of what you don't. Maybe you're trying to get the CEO's attention, but the only reason you do is because you're always Last-Minute Larry. Try being First-Minute Larry, not once but every time.

A Personal Action Plan is present tense and describes specific actions: "I will arrive at work fifteen minutes early . . . I will eliminate wasteful office chitchat . . . I'm going to take a class in time management . . ."

MY PERSONAL ACTION PLAN

_____

_____

_____

_____

BELIEF

To achieve the mind-set a person needs for daily peak performance and high-level achievement means incorporating a belief system into your quest for success.

Beliefs have tremendous power and can be used for good or ill, but either way, they affect people on a massive scale. Just look at the crazy and good things people do in the context of beliefs. Think of Adolf Hitler and the destruction caused by his singular belief in a superior race—his own. Think of Dr. Martin Luther King Jr. and the good he caused by his belief in equality.

You and I harbor beliefs about ourselves: some are empowering, others are limiting, and some are downright crazy. Your beliefs activate subconscious processes that can enslave you or serve you. They can unleash your talents to achieve greater heights or they can undermine your dreams and cripple your efforts, keeping you from giving your best.

Past failures can create an endless loop of negative beliefs that paralyze creativity and drive. A negative belief could be inflicted by a teacher's thoughtless aside, a coach's criticism or even by otherwise well-meaning parents. The eighth-grade teacher who made you feel dumb for asking a certain question might later be blamed for you being unwilling to speak up in college, that one stray comment causing you to believe it's just a matter of time before you look stupid again. Who wants to risk that?

A basketball coach of mine once told a newspaper reporter that I was the best athlete on his team and its top defender but not much of a shooter. I was seventeen years old and I had thought I could shoot until I read that.

Write down five positive beliefs you have about yourself. You can make your statements brief and positive, such as:

- "I am good with people."
- "I am disciplined."
- "I am good at math."
- "I am a great leader."

Now write yours here:

1. _____

2. _____

3. _____

4. _____

5. _____

Read them aloud with emotion and enthusiasm.

As you do, you will affirm these qualities and activate many changes in the body and the mind as endorphins and adrenaline are released. Images will flood your mind as old success patterns are reinforced and new pathways are primed. As your self-concept improves and your vision clears, your chance of success rises greatly. Controlling your beliefs will give you passion to succeed.

Negative Beliefs

Negative beliefs are often subtle, while on occasion they feel like a ten-ton ship's anchor tied around your neck, pulling you toward

Davy Jones's Locker. Either way, they limit your activity and may cause you to not even try.

I will never forget the original *Rocky* movie starring Sylvester Stallone and Talia Shire. Rocky tells his girlfriend, Adrian, that his parents said he didn't have much of a brain and he needed to use his body. She then tells him that everyone always told her that she didn't have much of a body and needed to use her brain. They both lived their lives accordingly until they met each other and both realized they were a little smarter (okay, in Rocky's case, not much!) and a little prettier than they were led to believe. Yet those youthful impressions stuck like Krazy Glue and played a large part in determining their future.

Sometimes, informal snap judgments and more official on-the-job ones, ranging from SAT/ACT scores to Myers-Briggs personality assessments, are used universally to interpret and measure our value in a negative way:

- "I am just average; look, my scores prove it!"
- "I am not pretty enough."
- "I am not good with numbers."
- "I am too old to learn something new."
- "I am not a good athlete."
- "I am not a good speaker. I get so nervous in crowds."
- "I am just not musically inclined and can't play an instrument."

The list goes on and on. There may be some truth to these beliefs, but they are not absolute. It's a good thing that "average" high school student Bob Bain and college *dropout* Bill Gates didn't buy into that one.

Being "average" is not a disease, and if it's the best you can do, fine! But only you determine how far you go. *Nobody* in business cares about your GPA or SAT! They care about your results.

You can go through all these negative beliefs and always find contrary evidence of success. Oprah Winfrey was not the most beautiful or smartest person on television, but she was just pretty and clever enough to outperform a lot of people who probably thought they were brighter than her and had seen more attractive talking heads.

Just because something is true of you doesn't mean it's a negative. The evidence told me I was not a great sprinter, but I took that to mean I might be pretty good at longer distances. Did I pout and complain about my slowness? After all, it was true! Or did I focus on what I *could* do?

Focus on the positive, root out and isolate the negative and look for contrary evidence. It's always there. Ask yourself: Is it true? And how can it benefit me? It benefits you by alerting you not to spend time doing things in which you have no chance of success. If you're five-two, you have no chance at being an NBA center. Change your direction.

The great physicist Stephen Hawking was given a negative belief based on which he should have died years ago from the debilitating effects of Lou Gehrig's disease (ALS). He refused to buy into it. The average person with ALS only lives for three years, and Hawking has lived more than forty in its clutches. There is always another way to look at and live life.

PAY THE PRICE

Ever since I started rock climbing, I have dreamed of climbing the face of El Capitan in Yosemite National Park. I rock climb whenever I can and harbor this recurring exhortation in the back of my mind: "You can do it! Go climb El Cap!"

But I also realize I'd have to pay the price of becoming good enough to make the climb. It would mean thousands of hours of training and totally changing my body type from size and power to lean and enduring. At six feet, 225 pounds and a combination power lifter/Olympic lifter, I am not the typical climber. My 350-pound bench press will not get me up El Cap. I know a number of great big wall climbers such as Peter Croft (five-nine, 150 pounds), who blitzed up El Cap and Half Dome in a single day back in 1986 and set a speed record for El Cap—four hours, twenty minutes—in 1992, and Mark Tarrant, a freaky six-foot, 155-pound Spider-Man who still climbs at an elite level at age forty-five.

I know the effort they put forth to get there and how hard they worked. I have a good climbing foundation with a good work ethic. With enough time on the rock and the right training program, my dream is possible. But I know the price for this success and am not willing to pay it. I have commitments to my family and business that need my utmost attention so, for now at least, El Capitan will remain a dream.

Looking at your own Personal Action Plan, are you willing to pay the price to give it everything you've got? If you aren't, then your Desire Statement is not ready to become a goal. It's a wish, a hope, a dream—but not a goal. Your Desire Statement may be so compelling that you really do want it and the rewards outlined in your Reward Statement. But your Personal Action Plan will tell you precisely what the price of achievement is. It's now up to you to decide whether you're willing to pay it.

Some people have a real problem implementing their Personal Action Plan and subsequently stall when they realize how challenging it is to reach the next level of anything. Many want their results too quickly, grow impatient and throw in the towel. Some start out with the zeal of an evangelist, only to realize that talking and writing about it got them excited but committing to daily tasks takes self-discipline and sacrifice. They give up, never having reached their full potential.

The level of passion to succeed parallels the reaction of people in life-and-death situations. Some see their situation as hopeless, and their brains shut down and the body follows. They stop looking for answers after a single doctor tells them, "Chances are slim for a recovery."

Others in the very same situation muster all their mental capacity to question one expert's conclusion and find a way to survive. They contact other doctors and actively seek more favorable solutions.

VALUE LINKING

In this section I will share a powerful connector in the chain of success. I call it Value Linking.

Your true values will determine what you do with your time and your life. Your true values govern your thinking and action. It's difficult to remain happy and whole and go against your core values. Your values have power and give you much more than motivation.

My mom and dad are two of the most important people in my life. I always want to make them prouder of me. I will be a success because it's going to reflect kindly on my parents to show them that I respect and admire all the hard work they did to raise me. That's a value. Am I working for them? No. I am working *because* of them. I am driven because of that.

We all hear athletes say, "I want to thank the Lord for bringing me here." That's a value to that person. He will work harder because he is going to praise the Lord. Does the Lord really care about a sports competition in Pasadena? Whether or not he does, the point is, that's a value people have. They respect and admire somebody, so they want to make somebody proud.

They want to give their kids a better life. That's a value. These drivers give people tremendous power to take risks, to work harder than they ever thought possible, and I think that's missing in a lot of goals.

Some people, when they have these values, just don't know how to use them for power. A guy I know who told everyone how much he valued his job and family had been chronically late to work for years. Then he and his wife had a new baby, an infant who did not sleep well at night, howling when Dad needed his sleep. It made a bad problem so much worse. Instead of making changes in his daily habits so that he could get to work on time, this guy kept coming in late, and he got fired. The wife, the baby, the job—all the things he *said* he valued—weren't enough to shake him from his bad habits. Now he's out of work and everything he valued in life is at stake.

Oscar de la Hoya was training for the 1988 Summer Olympics in Seoul, South Korea, when his mother was diagnosed with cancer. His mom was the most important person in his life; there was no one and nothing he valued more. He told her he was going to win a gold medal for her, and his training took on new meaning. It was no longer for personal glory, country or fame—it was about something far more meaningful in his life . . . *Mom*.

In 1998, Arena Football League veteran quarterback Kurt Warner was out of football, bagging groceries, when he got the call from the St Louis Rams to pack his bags and report to NFL training camp. He hardly played that year as a third-string backup, but the following season, when starter Trent Green was injured in a preseason game, Warner stepped up. He came on strong, producing one of the best seasons a quarterback has ever had. He was named the NFL MVP for 1999 (he won it again in 2001), led the Rams to victory in Super Bowl XXXIV and was named the Super Bowl MVP. (A decade later, Warner took another team, the Arizona Cardinals, to Super Bowl XLIII.)

All the while, Warner stayed true to his values, his God and his family. If either was missing from the equation, he might have failed miserably. He later used his success to showcase through the media his story of the love of his family and his relationship with God.

When you start value linking, you say, "I've got my family, I've got my God, I've got my professor, I've got my mentor . . . ," and you will show you are thankful for all of these things.

One of my favorite quotes is "Our talent is a gift from God; how we use it shows our appreciation." There's a driver for you. Others might say, "My talent is a gift from my parents; how I use it shows my appreciation." If we keep that value in front of us and tie it to our Desire Statement, it will give us something extra.

Now, consider the ten most important things in your life. Jot them below as they come to you. There is no right or wrong here, just brutal honesty. Without truth you will not get the value out of this exercise. Don't fool yourself like these extreme examples:

- *Family* . . . but you are never home and cheat on your spouse with any number of lovers.
- *God* . . . but you don't go to church, don't pray and have committed multiple crimes.

You get the idea. These are "want to be" values because the author was not living them and therefore they had no power.

THE 10 MOST IMPORTANT THINGS IN MY LIFE

1. _____

2. _____

3. _____

4. _____

5. _____

6. _____

7. _____

8. _____

9. _____

10. _____

I was once hired by a father to help his struggling college student son. After getting to know the student a little, I had him write down his top ten and assured him that Dad would never see the list. Good thing!

Check it out:

1. Girls
2. Beer
3. Volleyball
4. Friends
5. My dog
6. Parents
7. Live music
8. Hanging out
9. School
10. Mexican food

My job was not to judge but to help. I asked him to then prioritize the list. "Go back through and really think about your true values," I said, "and determine what order they are really in."

He went back and this time put his parents in front of his dog.

I said, "Mike, are you sure?" and he said, "Yes, it was close, but my parents are *definitely* ahead of the dog."

Clearly, I had some work to do. Dad didn't want any more bad grades or he would stop paying for school and all that went with it. Mike didn't want that.

The solution? I linked his values to the need for better grades. I made it clear that Dad was pulling him from college if his grades didn't improve, and he agreed he wanted to stay in school and graduate and go on to law school.

Girls and having fun were important to Mike; let's not deny it. His mom would have wanted to see God, family, country and school atop his values, but you have to work with what is there. I asked him if he would like to continue having fun, playing ball, graduating and making his parents proud. He was all for it.

I said, "Let's use your list to make sure you get what you want out of college and still make your parents proud. The key is to link your higher values to what your goal is. If you flunk out of school, what will your friends think? How will you meet girls from all over the country?"

This last question was the one that got his attention; now he was listening.

"Mike, how disappointed will your parents feel when they have to tell friends, 'Mike flunked out of college'? Let's take this goal of graduating and link your smiling proud parents to the outcome, add the respect of your friends as they see a fun-loving guy that can still get the job done. And we all know that girls love a winner."

We set his goal, linked his values, visualized the outcome, and twenty-five years later he is a practicing attorney . . . who still enjoys beer, women and fun!

Now, it's your turn. Take a look at your values and put them in a priority list as they truly are in your life right now. Ideally, the ones on which you set the highest priority are the most important, but any can be linked to your goal to give you more drive.

Rewrite your Desire and Reward Statements using "I will . . ." and incorporate your values into the reward. In Mike's case, the statements looked like this:

I will graduate on time, be accepted to law school and show my parents how much I appreciate what they have done for me. I can't wait to see the smile on my mom's face and my dad's nod of approval. My friends are important to me and I will work them in around my schooling, and I can't wait for the after-graduation volleyball party! I will pay the price and schedule fun around school.

Let your statement reflect your values and what's in your heart. Don't worry about whether it is grammatically correct, perfect in form or whether someone will disapprove. Let it flow and drive you to want to achieve it.

Here are two more examples:

I will be regional vice president by next fall and will have a motivated sales force. I will celebrate my success with NBA season tickets. I will buy my wife her dream house and start the kids' college fund. There is nothing in the world more important to me than my wife and kids. I will pay the price and learn to be a better leader.

I will make $80,000 this year and enjoy a Hawaiian vacation and learn to surf. The extra income will allow me to enjoy being healthy and learning new things. I will appreciate God's Creation and give glory to God. I will change for the better and focus on positive thoughts and will listen to the "Mental Edge Minute" to start my day.

SET THE MIND

Mindsetting is different than goal setting—a variation, if you will. There is nothing stronger than a made-up mind, and history proves it. Mahatma Gandhi and Dr. Martin Luther King Jr. underwent tremendous, life-threatening hardships because their minds were set on a goal. In a completely different arena, Bill Gates started Microsoft, made up his mind to compete against Apple and discovered a path to beating them.

Your Desire and Reward Statements will help you uncover what you really want. Your Personal Action Plan and your willingness to pay almost any price will determine whether success is or is not attainable for you. Mindsetting will help you "lock in" to your goals and "lock out" distractions, keeping your enthusiasm high. You will activate all of your mind's power to learn new skills faster and make needed changes.

Mindsetting will take your Desire Statement from "I want to" to the action state of "I will." This act alone will put you in the top tier of achievers, as most wannabes are stuck on "hoping to succeed" or are "giving it a try," inevitably leading to a less-than-best effort and partial success or massive failure. Most people go through life wishing and hoping things turn out for the best. But dreams are not achieved because of wishing and hoping. Rock-solid, well-thought-out goals are critical to keeping the mind and body working as one and recruiting all available resources for the achievement of the goal.

It's Time to Be SMART

Now that your mind is set, it's time to put these goals to work for you.

SMART goal setting is:

- **Specific.** Create Desire and Reward Statements and a Personal Action Plan that are as specific as possible. Make them clear—state *precisely* what you want to accomplish. You are better off saying, "I will increase sales 23 percent," than "I'd like to increase sales." With the clearest possible statement, your mind will know exactly what you want and it will call upon the resources you need to achieve your goal.

- **Measurable.** Keep track of your improvement; use it as a tool to make sure you are on pace. If you want to increase sales 23 percent, that is easy to monitor, and you should do so daily or weekly. Don't shy away from measurement, as it will show you that you're on the right track.

- **Attainable.** Your goal needs to be reachable, meaning that you must be willing to pay the price to hit it and you must have the necessary skills. If you are unwilling to make the sacrifice—making more sales calls, following up every lead— you may not have the mind-set to reach your goal.

- **Realistic.** Improving sales 23 percent is achievable. But if you set your goal to 1,000 percent, that's probably *not* going to happen and you will shut down and look for excuses. Ask yourself, "Has anyone achieved this before?" Evaluate your current numbers, your talent, strengths and weaknesses, and compare them to other successful, high-achieving salespeople. Keep in mind that just because it hasn't been done before doesn't mean it can't be done. Just ask Sir Roger Bannister, the runner of the first four-minute mile.

- **Time.** NBA Basketball Hall of Fame player Jerry West once told me that "having a goal without a deadline is like having a race with no finish line. It doesn't make sense." And I agree. Set a time frame in which to achieve your goals. If you plan to increase sales by 23 percent, is that for the week, the month or the year? Whatever the time frame picked, it must be well thought out and meaningful. How long do you really need to increase sales by 23 percent? Push yourself and monitor results as if this date is cast in stone.

Many people don't like to monitor results or keep score—just as some want to lose weight but don't want to step foot on the scale. Instead of motivating them, it makes them feel bad when they fail. A mind *not* made up or not desiring feedback is a recipe for failure.

Now that you have rock-solid goals, allow yourself to be driven by your Desire and Reward Statements. Read and reread the Personal Action Plan that you now possess. Then look back over your time frame, picturing yourself overcoming obstacles along the way, and enjoy the process of living your dream and turning it into a reality.

4

Rewire Your Brain

A friend of mine named Jimmy forms and finishes concrete for a living. He is always happy and enthusiastic; he loves life. The guys on his crew, on the other hand, are always pissing and moaning and complaining.

I asked him one day, "What is it about you that keeps you so up all the time?"

He said, "I don't pretend I don't lay concrete. Because in my mind, I build Los Angeles, and that's the way I look at it. I go to work every day to build the greatest city in the world."

Jimmy rewired his brain and took in all kinds of different stimuli. He was in the same exact job as everybody else, but he looked at it completely differently. As a result, he had this winner's attitude.

Being a winner does not mean being the richest person or having the biggest house. There is nothing wrong with being a concrete finisher. There is nothing wrong with being a secretary or a janitor.

Winning is having the mind-set, the Mind Over Business, that allows you to enjoy and embrace that activity and make your life great. Even though other people may see you as totally average, it doesn't mean you are.

Life is a mind game, and you make the rules.

I often say that to people I train. It's logical but foreign to most, as they really think that the way things are to them is the way things are to everyone. It's not uncommon to hear people say, "That's just the way I am." They go about their lives getting results they don't like, but they are unwilling to change behaviors because "it's just the way I am." They buy into limiting beliefs about themselves and society, and when someone breaks from the norm for a massive success, they shrug it off to luck or look for excuses as to why it happened to someone else but not to them.

It's also common to hear athletes talk of the other team's home field advantage and then play poorly, as if that were the cause.

My whole life I've heard, "It takes money to make money," as if there is no other way to make money except to have it first.

Are these beliefs true?

Former NBA star and Naismith Memorial Basketball Hall of Famer Charles Barkley consistently turned the other team's home court into *his* advantage by virtue of his mind-set. Home court advantage is real, but teams win in either team's home court all the time. It's not an absolute unless mentally you make it one. As for Barkley, he believed they were all against him (that's true!) and he would make them pay.

Three-time Super Bowl quarterback Tom Brady of the New England Patriots is like a surgeon regardless of whose field he is on.

He believes that with proper preparation, any team is beatable on any field on any given day. The NFL is a mind game and his mind makes the rules.

As for "It takes money to make money"?

Aleksander came to the United States from Poland without a penny to his name. He spoke little practical English and exuded an abrasive personality. He took a job driving an airport van, but his tips were terrible! He thought it must be because of his poor language skills, so he worked on his English—but his gratuities from passengers remained measly.

Perplexed, he asked one of his fares what he thought about his service as a driver.

The response was: "You are not a nice guy and you are rude."

Aleksander was hurt by this blunt appraisal.

"How could you think that? I am the *nicest* guy!" he proclaimed.

"Trust me on this, Aleksander," the passenger said. "I am in the people business and *you* are turning people *off*."

Aleksander thought he excelled at being fast and efficient, but all his clients saw was a cold, hard foreigner who treated them like mindless cattle. He absorbed and then shook off the hurt, then decided to do something about it. He bought a copy of the old Dale Carnegie standby, *How to Win Friends and Influence People*, and he read it from cover to cover. Following its many nuggets of wonderful advice, Aleksander modified his professional persona, and the tips started pouring in.

He lived frugally, saved his money and worked overtime whenever possible so he could save even more. He eventually bought an old van, applied for and received his own vanpool/taxi permit and started his own business. When I met him, Aleksander had five vans and ran a thriving business. He was shocked at how few

Americans he met saw the opportunities that he saw and took advantage of the free enterprise system the way he, a once-poor immigrant, had.

We all have the power to change on any scale. Every job can be an adventure and lead to a happy, fulfilled life. It's all about your attitude. Little changes like the ones that Aleksander made created a world of difference in his income and his enjoyment in getting his job done. (It also converted a job into a *career*.)

I Am What I *Think* I Am

Most people set their personalities in their teens and hone them during their early twenties. At that point, they stop changing and lock into a "this is the way I am" mind-set even if they don't express it. Habits become ingrained, and actions and responses are predictable. The thought of change becomes a chore and an admission that they have been wrong about living their life. "Better to be miserable than to admit I am wrong" is how many people live.

But it doesn't have to be that way. Change is healthy; change is good. I have a beautiful, smart, kind, athletic, loving daughter, Brittany (I can't help gushing!) who has been on the quiet side around groups of people since she was fourteen years old. Yet she could speak up in class, give a great speech without being nervous and be a quiet leader on her volleyball team.

Her mother would encourage her to speak up and not be so shy around boys. She just couldn't do it—until she was ready.

I told her, "Don't worry about it, but understand there is always a payoff for how we act. It could be boys will stay away, taking your shyness for being aloof. People that don't know you might never get to know you because you might seem uninterested if you don't converse."

Finally, the time was right and she changed in a way that was effective for her. She had read books and listened to audio programs I would recommend throughout the years, and finally, it all kicked in. I wasn't surprised. I myself was quite shy all through high school, too afraid to ask girls out on dates and scared to death in Mrs. Abbott's tenth-grade English class—*almost failing!*—because I couldn't gather the courage to give a required speech. I kept putting the speech off, and finally Mrs. Abbott said, "If you don't give the speech, you can't play basketball." I *lived* to play basketball, so I finally gave the speech. But I was petrified and said to myself, "I will never do this again!"

I realized later that I was just as valuable, as important, as anybody else. But until then I felt inferior and afraid to make a mistake, afraid to look bad, afraid that people would laugh at me. Then I discovered it didn't matter. A message has to get across. If you are going to sell for a living, whether it's one-on-one or in a group, if you are going to train people, you have to get the job done. You can't worry about mistakes—everybody makes them—so I just changed my mind-set.

Today, I give speeches all over the world to small groups and in fourteen-thousand-seat arenas, a development made possible when I overcame that early fear.

Everybody has the capacity to change. It just takes humility, sometimes pride, and an "I will" attitude.

The resources that can trigger change are all around us. My mom had an eighth-grade education because her mother died when she was fourteen and she had to stay home and raise her younger brother and sister. She bounced around from one grade school to another and missed a lot of days as her family relocated from place to place. She had difficulty reading, and her writing was poor. I remember her taking me to the Buena Park Library when I was thirteen years old because she wanted to change her life and she just knew there must be a way in the library's books to do it. She would check out a stack of books at a time and read them—slowly. Some she couldn't understand, but she was committed to changing. She told me, "Everything you want to learn can be found at the library." I never forgot that, and when I was twenty-three, I decided it was time to find something better in my life instead of lousy odd jobs. I haunted our local library and bookstores and read hundreds of books over the next few years. I sometimes read two or three books in a day while standing in the bookstore stacks. What I learned in the process drastically changed my life: Life is a mind game, and *you* make the rules.

If you are not winning the game, *rewrite the rules*! It's your game; you are captain of the team, quarterback or owner (and sometimes janitor)! Nobody can stop you but you!

Many people once believed in the Tooth Fairy and/or Santa Claus. One year, I remember a neighbor boy and I were playing in his garage a few weeks before Christmas. I was in second grade and he was in third grade, but I was the one who no longer believed in Santa. I told my friend, "There is no Santa—your *parents* buy the presents on Christmas!"

He turned beet red with anger.

"There is *too* a Santa! My parents wouldn't lie to me!"

Ooops.

Boy, was I in trouble. You do not want to be the neighborhood kid who destroys the dreams of your entire generation, let me tell you. His mom called my mom on the phone and chewed her out. Then my mom gave me an earful. My friend's mother knew it wasn't time yet for him to change.

Sometimes, despite all evidence to the contrary, we hold on to our original self as if the original self is better than a progressive self. Many people hold on to lack of change like a badge of honor instead of the lead weight it really is. Most people logically realize it's not possible for a fat man in a red suit to be led by a dozen reindeer to deliver presents to the whole world. Their views evolve as they mature. They don't turn beet red and throw a tantrum . . . until it comes to performance reviews. "What do you mean I need to work faster? I work as fast as So-and-So; how come you are not picking on him?"

Salespeople have the tendency to fortune-tell others' responses, and that's where the fear of cold-calling arises. I used to tell my Mental Edge clients, "When you see a 'No Soliciting' sign on a door, it means they're weak, that they're probably going to buy from you, and they had to put up the sign so that you won't come in, because they will buy almost anything you're selling." It's *your* game. Who makes the rules? You do. So when you see that sign, say, "I notice you have a 'No Soliciting' sign, so I am just dropping something off for free that will help you," and that's the way you change that perception.

Are you ready to face reality and change?

|||||||||||||||||||||||||||||||||||||||||||| **E X E R C I S E** ||||||||||||||||||||||||||||||||||||||||||||

WRITE DOWN 5 LIMITING BELIEFS
YOU HAVE ABOUT YOURSELF

||||||||||||||||||||||||||||||||||||||||||||||||||||||||||||||||||||||||||||||||||||||||||||||||||||||||||||||

Here are some examples to get you started:

I'm not educated enough.

I'm not a good networker.

I'm not good-looking enough.

Selling is beneath me.

_____

_____

_____

_____

_____

Is there any evidence that any or all of these may not be true?

_____

How did you develop these beliefs?

_____

Are they keeping you from getting what you want out of business, friendships or other relationships?

_____

If so, what can you do to change them?

_____

Who can you talk to about this? What can you read or listen to? How can you defocus a belief and limit its negative impact?

_____

||||||||||||||||||||||||||||||||||||||||||||||||||||||||||||||||||||||||||||||||||||||||||||||||||||||||||||||||

||||||||||||||||||||||||||||||||| **EXERCISE** |||||||||||||||||||||||||||||||||||||

WRITE DOWN 5 POSITIVE BELIEFS
YOU HAVE ABOUT YOURSELF

||||||||||||||||||||||||||||||||||||||||||||||||||||||||||||||||||||||||||||||||||||||||||||||||||||||||||||||||

Here are some examples to get you started:

I am smart.

I am good with math.

I am likeable.

I look good.

_____

_____

_____

_____

_____

How can you use these beliefs more effectively?

_____

One thing you can do is use a positive to flush out a negative. Imagine holding a glass of dirty water under a running faucet and letting clean water run into it. It displaces the dirty water, right? Do you let the water drip a little at a time or open the faucet full force? The size of the glass, the dirtiness of the water and the inflow rate of clean water determines the rate of displacement. How much negativity is in your life and how long it has affected you will determine how long it will take to flush it out.

Pay Attention and Learn!

One of the best ways to tap into your power to grow is to talk to older, successful businesspeople and get their feedback. Keep your ego and judgment at bay. Listen, learn and do. Donald Trump and Ted Turner are vastly different people, but they will each tell you the same ingredients are needed for success. Donald Trump, for example, says that before he goes into a deal, he asks himself, "What is the worst thing that can happen if this fails?" If he can live with that outcome, he moves forward 100 percent committed to success. If you keep hearing the same things over and over from different trusted sources, maybe you might want to give their advice a try.

Turner said something complementary: "I have never run into a guy who could win at the top level in anything today and didn't have the right attitude, didn't give it everything he had, at least while he was doing it; wasn't prepared and didn't have the whole program worked out."

I always ask my cocky young martial arts students and athletes, "Who knows more—a four-year-old or a nine-year-old?" It's always, hands down, unanimously, the nine-year-old. So then I ask them, "Who knows more, a nine-year-old or a thirteen-year-old?"

Once again everyone gets it right: the thirteen-year-old. I ask, "Who knows more—a thirteen-year-old or an eighteen-year-old?" And they always agree on the eighteen-year-old. I ask, "Who knows more, an eighteen-year-old or a fifty-year-old?" and they get it: Sensei has been doing this a lot longer than they have been alive, so he might know a thing or two. *Pay attention and learn!* When we are adults this is harder to do, because we have already acquired some knowledge, life experience and our own settled ways of seeing and doing things.

I learned fly-fishing in Banff, Alberta, Canada, alongside my daughter and son. One morning as we waited for our fishing guide outside a bait and tackle store, a man drove up in a nice Jeep. He was dressed like our vision of the perfect guide, ready to be photographed for the cover of *Field & Stream*. We were excited to meet him and get started on our family adventure, but he walked past us to a car parked a few spaces over to meet someone else.

It was getting late and our guide was still nowhere to be found. We were all pretty antsy when a big ol', smoke-chuggin' white Dodge van pulled up and out stepped Scotty. His untamed hair was sticking out of a tattered floppy hat. He was squeezed into tight coveralls that were two sizes too small. Oh, and he wore what looked like his grandmother's house slippers.

We looked at each other and thought, "Nope, that can't be our guide—can it?"

He came over to our car and cheerfully introduced himself. He changed from slippers to boots, and off we stomped toward the river. All along the way, Scotty described what we saw in great detail, picking us delicious wild berries to eat and warning us of local bear behavior. He found a spot along the river and rigged up the kids' gear. I was on my own and the kids had him.

I didn't like the looks of the first spot he suggested, so I went off to find another. After all, I had caught a few fish in my day and thought I could read a river pretty well.

Soon I heard my kids "woo-hoo"ing as they pulled out fish after fish with guidance from the great Scotty. *I* wasn't catching anything. But I refused to rejoin the group. I knew how to fish. But the "woo-hoo"ing was deafening; even the fish knew I was defeated. My desire to catch fish overtook my pride, and I let Scotty teach me a thing or two. As my kids and I learned . . . Scotty the Guide knew fishing!

Just because we know a little or a lot doesn't mean we can't learn. Scotty fishes 350 days a year. When Canada gets too cold, he fishes off the Baja California peninsula and then returns to Canada when the Great White North warms up. There are a lot of Scottys out there that can help you to change and grow even though they may not look the expected part of Sensei. But Scotty, he knows fish.

The Power of Perception

One of life's great lessons is that perception is your "lock on" or key to success.

Our perceptions shape our world and cause us to be who we are. When we take control and decide to change, we must take stock of how we look at things or we will continue our current course of thought and action and our lives will not change. Our perceptions shape our world and create our own unique reality. That's exciting because, with a few simple tweaks and Consistent Resilient Action, we can change our world and the opportunities in it.

Many people have perceptions that doom them to failure. They often present themselves as self-righteous, justifying their outlook by the way the cards just didn't play out for them. We hear it all the time:

- "I didn't go to college, so I can't compete."
- "It's not *what* you know, it's *who* you know."
- "I can't follow my dream because I have a family."
- "It takes money to make money."
- "I would do that, but . . ."

The list of excuses goes on and on.

The people we choose to follow form our perceptions, as do the books we read, the music we hear and the entertainment choices we make. Perceptions may also be influenced by wild cards that we can't always control, such as religion and family history.

Little things can make lasting impressions and shape a person's life forever. Maybe it's a famous quotation that really speaks to us and motivates us to do great things. Or it could be a grandparent we love dearly who says, without equivocation, "I expect you to do great things!"

But it's not always for good. One of my uncles told his son, "You are not smart enough to do anything special, so just get a job," and sure enough, he bought into that one stupid comment and never let go of it. Worse than even that—or maybe because of it—the son blundered his whole life away and died at thirty-seven from a drug overdose. He went through his entire short life feeling like he was ugly, stupid and a good-for-nothing loser.

In my youth, I remember hearing my uncles and cousins always complaining because they couldn't find a job. I remember older cousins and some uncles coming back from a job search and saying,

"Nobody is hiring." They drew unemployment checks, and miraculously, when their unemployment ran out, they would find a job, work long enough to max out their next round of government subsidy, get fired and start the cycle all over again.

Someone I respected used to say, "There is always a job if you want to work."

These were the dueling points of view with which I was raised. *Which one do I choose? What life do I want?* I took stock of the lives of both, and it was easy to choose. I started doing lawn work in third grade, had a paper route in fourth grade, cleaned parking lots in fifth grade, worked at a neighborhood pizza parlor from eighth to tenth grade and pumped gas from tenth through twelfth grade. I *never* had trouble finding a job my whole life. I saw through my cousins' and uncles' limited perceptions of the world around them and decided to follow one of my own: "There is always a job if you want to work."

Too often, people from all kinds of backgrounds think in ways that limit their potential before they even try. Their attitude—not their education, skin color or sex—is the problem. They are just not willing to use their minds to break free from limited thinking and stretch themselves to maximize the potential they possess.

In the next section I will share with you ten Perception Stretchers. They will help you change your thinking about what is possible for you in business and in life. They will help to counter any limiting perceptions you may have about yourself. They will expand your vision and help you prepare for the success that will come your way.

By applying these perception stretchers to your daily life, you'll alter your thinking and develop a mind-set to take full advantage of all the techniques in this book.

Let's get started!

10 PERCEPTION STRETCHERS

1. Attitude Is Everything

I left home to take an entry-level position, living out my first dream, working for the U.S. Forestry Service. I was one of six people in a truck of new recruits driving to Meeks Bay in Lake Tahoe. It was the middle of winter, freezing cold, with blowing snow and a wind-chill factor of fifteen degrees. Everyone in the truck complained about the cold and the fact that we had to go out in it—everyone except JoAnne. As everyone around her was whining, JoAnne spoke up loudly and flashed a big wide grin. "It's always a great day at Meeks Bay," she told us. Everyone looked at her and laughed; we thought she was crazy. I never forgot that moment—what she said, and the bright, cheerful attitude that went with it. She was right. The weather didn't change the beauty of Meeks Bay. It was a remarkable place, and the elements just added to the challenge of building a much-needed fence.

If you visit my BioDynamax Training Center, you can't miss the sign I posted that says: *Attitude Is Everything*. It is the one thing I make sure everyone knows how to apply. Only *you* can make today a good day or a bad day. It's the great equalizer, and everyone on the planet has control of his or her attitude—if they so choose.

2. Limitations Are Temporary

When I first started training athletes, I myself had many limitations. I just didn't know it yet. My lack of a degree didn't bother me, and I forged ahead oblivious to its importance to anyone else. Nothing could stop me because I had made up my mind to do this. When players, teams or news reporters would ask me where I got my sports psychology degree, I would say, "I don't have one, I have *results*!" For many, that was enough. But for others, it was not the answer they sought, and I lost many a job or interview because of it.

For some aspiring sports psychologists, it would be devastating to have their credentials questioned, but I kept going, researching, studying and helping athletes. I have also written three books. Not bad for a high school dropout and a solid C English student without a college degree.

Limitations are temporary when you take the needed action to turn them into strengths. Don't worry about what you don't have; *do* with what is yours. Don't let *your* limitations keep you from living out your dreams.

3. Knowledge Is a Treasure Chest; Action Is the Key

Susan was a yoga and Pilates instructor. She was educated, pretty and incredibly competitive but afraid to leave her comfort zone. "If only I knew a little more," she told me, and then she put off teaching to pursue the next certification or sign up for another class.

After one of many conversations with her, I asked, "When is enough education enough?"

She replied, "I'm not sure, but I need to know this inside and out so I don't look bad if I don't know something."

"Think of all the people you are not helping right now because you are afraid someone might ask a question to which you don't know the answer," I said. "You are one of the fittest, nicest, most well-informed yoga/Pilates instructors there is, but you're not helping anyone! You need to go out and start helping people right now! They need you, and you will make their lives better. Yoga is not brain surgery!"

Take the steps to get started on your life, know what you need to know to begin and learn the rest as you move on. You will never know it all, but be open to knowing all that is needed to at least *start*.

Nate Walton had a plan. He would go to the finest schools he could get into and build a sterling educational résumé that would open doors to the most successful people and companies. He graduated from Princeton University and earned an MBA from Stanford. Then he went on vacation for two years.

His dad, the legendary basketball player Bill Walton, joked with Nate, "I gave you the best education money can buy and you can't even get a job?"

Nate knew knowledge was a treasure chest; he was resting up for the Herculean effort that was yet to come. He charted his course. He just needed some time to know which key would open that chest. Today he works for a large hedge fund in Los Angeles while managing business deals for his brother, L.A. Laker Luke Walton, and other professional athletes.

Don't waste *your* time trying the wrong keys. Educate toward your strengths, forge the right key and, when it's time, give it a 100 percent turn.

4. Habits Create Consistent Results

Take stock of where you stand in business and life. If you don't like what you see, it's time to do something different.

The challenge is that we get comfortable being who we are and quickly land in a bit of a rut. If the rut gets deep enough, after so many years, the rut becomes a grave. We are stuck going nowhere, repeating the same daily routines, wondering why things don't get better for us. "Why didn't I get the promotion?" "Why doesn't my business do better?"

Changing little things can create big results:

- Get to the office ten minutes early.
- Talk to two new people a day.
- Read or listen to something educational or motivational about your profession during breakfast.
- Take five minutes a day to organize your work area.

Chuck, an advertising sales rep, tried my advice and approached two more potential clients a day for six weeks. The result? Eight minutes of work was added to his workday, and in six weeks, he contacted sixty new people, had nine new sales and added commissions of $948. You are the result of your habits.

5. A Loss Becomes a Gain

Lloyd had a janitorial service. It was a thriving business, and it never occurred to him that his main client might let him go, but one sad day, that's exactly what happened.

As a result, Lloyd's business crumbled and he was forced to get a regular job. Lacking any high-value business or technical skills, he took a job in the mailroom with a new Internet-based company. As only the seventh employee of this growing company, he didn't think too much about his stock options, figuring he would never be there long enough because he planned to eventually rebuild his janitorial service, and the online stock trading service company would probably go under first anyway.

Boy, was Lloyd wrong! His humble mailroom job turned him into a millionaire—twelve times over—as the company went ballistic. He was in the right place at the right time; the company went public, he cashed in, and the account loss became the greatest thing that ever happened to him, opening the door to a huge gain working for someone else. And he never went beyond the mailroom.

It's true: when one door closes, another door opens, but you may have to do a lot of knocking to find the right one.

When my best friend committed suicide in high school, it was a terrible tragedy. Nothing good came out of it at the time. But it got me interested in why people do what they do, and I began an in-depth, practical study of psychology that helped me to change and in turn help many others to change.

You never know when or where tragedy will strike. How you react determines if the loss can become a gain. Ponzi schemes happen, business failures happen; your reaction can make it a positive life changer or a depressing life waster.

The lesson? Don't be a whiner! Lick your wounds and move forward. Learn from even your negative experiences and turn them into something great.

6. Imagination Is More Powerful Than Willpower

Nikolai Tesla is generally credited with the invention of fluorescent lighting, the Tesla induction motor and the Tesla coil, and for developing the alternating current (AC) electrical supply system, which included a motor and transformer, and three-phase electricity. He was one of the greatest inventors in history, but Tesla never willed his way to anything—he imagined it. He had a unique ability to see images and complex designs clearly in his mind.

When Mark Zuckerberg created the social networking site Facebook as an improvement on something called the "Harvard Connection," he imagined a concept and saw the coding necessary to build it. Today there are more than 500 million Facebook users and Zuckerberg is one of the world's youngest and most influential billionaires ever. As illustrated in the movie *The Social Network*, the Winklevoss twins—the students who envisioned the Harvard Connection that triggered the creation of Facebook—had willpower, and what did they come up with? Nothing, because they didn't have the *imagination*. Zuckerberg had the imagination *and* the willpower. That's where the real power comes together. The Winklevoss twins had nothing but willpower, and they tried to bring in the right people—such as Zuckerberg—to make it happen. And without his imagination, we wouldn't have Facebook.

Once the imagination does its thing—a kind of mental adrenaline—willpower kicks in to see us through. Let your mind find new ways of doing things, of being creative. Willpower alone isn't enough. You need imagination and ability ahead of willpower. You have an imagination; let it flow freely the way Tesla and Zuckerberg did, regardless of what others think.

7. Success Leaves Clues

Let's assume for a moment that every person that reads this book wants to improve his or her performance quickly but doesn't know how.

One effective technique for performing better is to pattern yourself after the excellence of others. Find an outstanding businessperson who performs in a way you respect and admire. Break down his or her skills into steps that will create a pattern for you to follow. Visualize yourself becoming more like that person. See a better performance by picturing yourself precisely the way you want to be as you blend your talent with someone else's. To become more like your role model, don't question or judge, just *do*.

If you are not a good carpenter but still want to build a cabinet, ask a lot of questions of the lumber guys at the Home Depot, get a good set of plans and follow them.

I remember once going into a Texas barbecue restaurant on Pacific Coast Highway in California, at a location that was notorious for being the home of numerous failed restaurant concepts. Upon entering, I immediately wanted to walk right back out. But I was intrigued enough to stay and puzzle it out. The hostess was from the Middle East and spoke with an accent to match. She walked me to my table, and I saw a floor covered, literally, with about four inches of sawdust. The décor was also odd, spotlighting aspects of Texas, of course, but also California and the Middle East. The waiters were all Middle Eastern. They brought out a bucket of peanuts with the menus and told us to just throw the shells on the floor. All I could think of was "How do they clean a floor covered in peanut shells and so much sawdust?" But the menu read well, and its appetizing photos and description of the plates made me hungrier. Still, I worried that because there was not a Texan in sight, the BBQ probably wouldn't be any good. And I was right. The food was cold, the sides were small, and they served Middle Eastern bread instead of cornbread, biscuits or Texas toast. Sure enough, a few short months later they were out of business because they did not pattern their restaurant on a successful Texas BBQ.

Suppose you're a restaurant owner and you are teetering on the verge of success. Find a restaurant similar to yours and figure out what makes it successful. Look at its menu, pricing, décor, relationship building, order taking and how the staff answers the phones; sample the food, investigate the restaurant's advertising, ordering and inventory practices, what they pay the help and even the way they bus the tables, and you will get all the answers you need to start the steady climb toward success of your own. You will be surprised how many successful people will gladly tell you their story and lend a guiding hand.

8. Events Have No Meaning Except That Which You Give Them

Black Monday—October 19, 1987—was the day the American stock market took a precipitous dive unseen in several generations and thousands of people panicked. One disgruntled investor walked into his broker's office and shot the poor man to death. Others demanded their money back, took a loss and put their money in CDs and under mattresses. Perception, not reality, was king that day!

A little more than a year later the market rebounded and went on a tremendous run. Black Monday was nothing more than the prelude to that remarkable ride. If you sold that day in a panic, however, it's still Black Monday to you because you forever lost your shirt. You overreacted.

Pete Carroll was fired as head coach of the New England Patriots in 1999 because he wasn't winning. He was perceived as a loser by fans and the team's management. But he didn't buy in. He took the opportunity of being fired on the East Coast to accept a more suitable opportunity and became one of the most successful college coaches in history on the West Coast over the next decade, winning two National Championships at the University of Southern California (USC). *He* didn't label himself a loser.

9. The More You Expect from a Situation, the More You Will Achieve

Positive expectations breed enthusiasm and extra effort. I shouldn't tell you this story, but the point is so good . . . Sorry, Harry!

I was training a group to hike Mount Whitney, the highest peak in the forty-eight states. In preparation, we did a training trip up to an elevation of nine thousand feet. As we began, a few hikers more used to being at sea level started sucking wind.

As we progressed, it became an increasingly strenuous climb, and I casually said, "There is a 7-Eleven at the top where you can get a Slurpee." I didn't expect anyone would *believe* me—it was a joke!—but Harry and Lisset did.

Soon it was just a quarter mile to the top, and I decided I would run to get in some extra cardio work. I excused myself and took off with Harry right behind me. I said, "Harry, you really shouldn't run. This gets pretty extreme," but he stayed with me for a bit and then disappeared.

I arrived at the top and enjoyed the spectacular views and met a few other hikers. A few minutes later, Harry came charging up the mountain, panting, and he said—I swear this is true—"Where is the 7-Eleven, Ken?"

"On the other side of the Ranger Tower," I replied with as straight a face as I could manage.

Understand we were a good fifty miles from any 7-Eleven, on a rugged trail that no vehicle—let alone most individuals—could manage. But Harry started taking orders and asked me what I wanted.

I was dying inside!

Lisset arrived and announced that she needed a Slurpee in the worst way possible. She dug in her backpack for money and followed Harry to the other side of the Ranger Tower on the mountain peak. When they saw the hikers from another group, they asked earnestly, "Where is the 7-Eleven?"

Unable to hold it in another moment, I burst out laughing. In fact, our entire group was convulsed in laughter. It was awesome. But then I felt bad. Harry said he guzzled all his water two miles back so he wouldn't have to carry any and started to run so he could get hydrated faster. Harry *really* wanted a Slurpee! He had an expectation, and it caused him to move faster than he'd ever thought possible.

The more you expect from a situation, the more you will give. Harry thought he was going to get a Slurpee, so he put more effort into it. If he hadn't thought the Slurpee was waiting for him, he would have gone slower, he would have had a different attitude. His expectancy of that reward at the end gave him extra motivation. Anytime we expect something good, we will be successful. It changes our attitude, it changes our whole mind-set, posture, breathing—*everything*.

Plan for your Desire Statement to become a reality and expect to reap all the rewards from its achievement. (And conserve your water!)

10. There Is No Failure, Only Feedback

If you never fail, it means you never tried to stretch yourself or do anything of significance. We all fail sometime! If you don't, it means you are stuck in your comfort zone and your ego is keeping you from maximizing your potential.

If Michael Jordan had quit shooting after he missed his first game-winning shot, we wouldn't have had MJ. Instead, he realized that it's a game of percentages and that if he kept shooting, eventually he would win.

The only real failure is quitting. Once you quit, you have no chance at success.

Charles Goodyear invented the vulcanization of rubber so it wouldn't freeze in winter and turn to mush in summer. It took him more than five years of failed experiments and a little luck to get it right. He went broke, people he loved and respected turned their backs on him—he even went to jail—but he persevered against all odds, eventually earning a patent for his creation on June 15, 1844. Failure was feedback for him because he didn't quit—he used it to refine himself and his product.

5

Seeing Is Believing

James looked like a million bucks, with all the recognizable trappings of wealth. Alligator belt, Rolex watch, Armani pin-striped suit, and of course, you could always find him behind the wheel of the latest Mercedes-Benz.

His father had told him, "You need to *look* like a success before you can *be* a success. People are visual and they buy with their eyes." (I guess his dad wasn't familiar with billionaire Warren Buffett, who lives in a modest house and is anything but flashy.)

James couldn't open or close a door—let alone open or close a sale. While he had the look of the finest Swiss watch, on which European craftsmen carefully used their precise instruments, he was empty. Flash took the place of substance as his father's myth was perpetuated. It was like trying to turn a donkey into a Thoroughbred by wrapping its legs and putting on blinders. Even if you used the best leg wraps around, a donkey would still be a jackass.

It's true: visual impressions are valuable, but for long-term success, content is still king.

Somewhere along the way James had talked himself into his father's myth, and he accumulated the visual imagery and emotions to support it.

My job was to train James because the president of his company said, "He looks so good he has to be a huge success!" Indeed, he had passed the basic aptitude test and earned a college degree; he spoke well and, no doubt, he looked good. What more could you ask in a new hire?

Plenty, it turns out!

James had no drive, couldn't handle rejection, didn't like working on commission and wasn't fond of sales. And forget networking. Most of his friends were living the same lifestyle and had nothing to offer. He was taught how to use the phone to make contacts and get appointments, but he couldn't bring himself to pick up the phone and do the work. He was taught how to cold-call and present the product at free public events, but he couldn't bring himself to peddle his wares.

"People should come to me," he thought.

I couldn't figure how he thought people would find him until he said, "I always saw myself working in a bank or investment house where people sought me out." He wanted to be an in-house advisor. In his mind that was classy and professional. Sales were beneath him.

People are often in jobs where they don't belong. The great songwriter Woody Guthrie was once a sign painter, but that was never how he saw himself.

The way you see yourself is the truth for you regardless of aptitude tests or the impressions of others. Your self-image is the limit to your success—not the fancy clothes and bling you wear. You are what you think you are. That's a challenge because you can change how you see yourself and break through your current limitations. You can have your desire come true if it harmonizes with your self-image. If not, you will fail.

That leads me to visualization and self-actualization. Some of it is good, some of it is not so good, and some of it is flat-out ridiculous and harmful.

When I first learned about visualization, I was fourteen years old and read *They Call Me Coach*, a book by the legendary UCLA basketball coach John Wooden. In it, he describes how he would have ballplayers lie on the ground and visualize success. He would even have them visualize specific skills. I thought, if that technique is good enough for the mighty Bruins, I would give it a try. Try as I might, however, nothing happened.

As I got older, I had the opportunity to talk with a number of Coach Wooden's current and former players and discovered that some got great results from these horizontal sessions while others gained nothing more than a nice catnap. Why the difference? Because not everyone is highly visual and not everyone visualizes the same way.

I studied hundreds of self-help books and attended countless lectures and found that few people addressed these differences. Instead, they continued regurgitating the same myths: "Just believe and achieve," or "If you can see yourself doing it, you can do it." This overly general, naïve, one-philosophy-fits-all approach set up many people for failure. *The Secret* isn't really a secret at all, and there is much more to success than just visualizing or thinking positively. (Think about your favorite song and hear the singer's voice. Now visualize yourself singing just like her. Open your mouth and let 'er rip. Not the same, is it?)

When it comes to visualizing, we all do it to one degree or another. I trained thousands of athletes and businesspeople one-on-one, and studied hypnotherapy and other performance psychologies and neuro-linguistic programming—the language of your brain, an approach for making yourself a new person—and soon realized that everyone visualizes differently. What works for one person doesn't work for the next. But while one size won't fit everyone, there are some commonalities that apply to us all. We all see some type of imagery. We all have internal self-talk.

And there is a growing body of evidence that imagery can impact performance in business, school, sports and life. Here is a brief background on how visualization works:

The brain has two hemispheres, and you use both all the time. The left hemisphere utilizes logic and analysis, controlling our use of words for primary communications. During visualization, however, we rely much more on the right hemisphere, which is responsible for imagination and visual pictures. As you create images in your mind, you are actually linking both hemispheres and using all of the tools available to you to make your performance the best it can be.

Researchers have found that, in a real sense, visualizations put your body through the paces before you ever perform a skill or task. Vivid images can produce subtle but real firings along the neural pathways that participate in the physical activities that you are visualizing.

I have seen this firsthand as I watched businesspeople and athletes change their posture, breathing and thoughts based on what they see in their mind's eye. I watched a swimmer fire his muscles and breath as if he was actually swimming while sitting in a bleacher, then go into a pool and duplicate the visualization within a few hundredths of a second. I also witnessed a scared, tongue-tied, educated young lady with low self-esteem rise to the occasion and become a business leader when she learned to program her imagery for the actions needed for success.

During visualizations you are, in a sense, priming the body for a particular task ahead, whether it's firing an employee, presenting end-of-the-year account reports, or picking up the phone and cold-calling a prospective client. We condition our brain, nervous system and body to perform in the way we want them to, increasing our chance of success. This contributes to self-confidence. And it puts the brain and body in a new comfort zone that allows you to perform well.

Rewire Your Brain with Visualization

One of the best ways to reach a goal is to see yourself having achieved it and enjoying the rewards that go with it.

Try the following exercise and notice how it creates a certain level of excitement or passion. You may feel as if you are actually performing. You may hear sounds and experience smells and tastes and everything else in vivid detail, or your experience may be more muted. The idea is to feel everything you can as you go through this exercise; it will give you feedback as to how your mind works. You'll notice I ask many questions in the visualization process below. I do that to get you to find out how you visualize best. (TIP: You might find it easiest to do this exercise and others if someone reads the instructions to you.)

IIIIIIIIIIIIIIIIIIIIIIIIIIIIIIIIIIIIIIIIIIIIIII **E X E R C I S E** IIIIIIIIIIIIIIIIIIIIIIIIIIIIIIIIIIIIIIIIIIIIII
FUTURE PACE
IIIIIIIIIIIIIIIIIIIIIIIIIIIIIIIIIIIIIIIIIIIIIIIIIIIIIIIIIIIIIIIIIIIIIIIIIIIIIIIIIIIIIIIIIIIIIIIIIIIIIIIIIIIIIIIIIIII

Close your eyes, take a deep breath, exhale gently and breathe normally through the nose, back of the throat and gently in the belly. Let your chest go still; feel your belly rise and fall. Your forehead is smooth, your eyes are soft, your cheeks are loose, and your jaw is slack. Your lips are slightly separated. Calmly, purposefully, continue to breathe. After a few breaths, imagine your Desire Statement as having been achieved. Put yourself sometime in the future, when all your dedication and hard work has paid off. Become aware of the expression on your face; perhaps it's a big, proud smile or a calm, relaxed picture of contentment. Maybe your arms are outstretched in the air as if to say, "I did it!"

Notice your body posture. Is there confidence in your physical presence? Are you standing tall with your shoulders back? How are you breathing? What are you thinking now that your dream has become a reality? How do you interact with other people? How do other people interact with you? Think about whom you really want to share this achievement with. Notice how you feel inside and ask yourself this question as you enjoy the rewards of your accomplishment: Was it worth it? Was it worth the sacrifices and effort that got me here? If you decide it was, start working backward in time. What were some of the obstacles you had to overcome to achieve your goal? Notice the negative people you had to contend with, those that doubted you or thought you didn't have a chance.

Become aware of some of the beliefs you had about yourself that needed to change, some limits that you had to go beyond. Notice how focused you became about your goal. As you continue to work backward in time, think about where you were just a month before you started this quest, maybe even a year or two earlier, and notice again where you are now, having achieved your goal in a relatively short period of time. Allow yourself to feel good about what you've accomplished. Allow your mind, body and emotions to work together in harmony to make this happen.

This exercise gives you insight into how you visualize. Were the images clear in your mind? Were they like photographs or a movie? Did they fade in and out? Did you feel like you were *in* the movie, or watching the movie? Was the sound clear or dull? Did you hear your own voice or the sounds around you—or both? Did you feel like you were participating? Did you want to gesture or move or smile or make some other expression? Did you feel the satisfaction? No matter your experience, together we will heighten your abilities to make your visualizations powerful and life-changing. The following powerful exercise shows just one way in which visualization can be used.

EXERCISE
THE LEMON

This exercise illustrates the power of visualization while using all five senses.

Sit down and relax. Take a deep breath and exhale forcefully. Breathe normally and, after a few breaths, imagine going to your refrigerator and grabbing a lemon. In which hand do you feel it? Notice the texture of the skin as you roll it around in your hand. Notice the smell as you bring it close to your nose. Set it on the counter or table. Notice what the lemon looks like on the counter. See the contrast in colors? Now feel yourself open a drawer and pick up a sharp knife. Become aware of the sounds you hear. What does the knife feel like in your hand? Grab the lemon and position it on the counter to be cut in half. Notice how you hold the lemon and the knife. What motion will you use to cut it? Set the knife on top of the lemon and slice through. What are the sounds you hear as the knife goes through the fruit? Feel the spray and aroma as the knife is cutting. Notice the sound as it breaks through the membrane and hits the counter. Smell the juice as the lemon falls apart in two halves. What does the lemon look like inside? Pick up one half of the lemon, tilt your head back and squeeze the lemon into your mouth.

This exercise shows how the body reacts to visual imagery and how this reaction is intensified when you use all five senses. This is how you want to visualize your business success. Make it so real that the body has to react viscerally. It is these very reactions that create muscle movements and physiological shifts, some out of your conscious awareness—like flaring nostrils or more subtle facial or breathing changes—that ultimately create reality, even though what you started with was just an image.

When you attempt this type of full-blown imagery to acquire new skills, you will learn faster, guaranteed, because you prepare the body in advance for what is expected and your brain gives your body a path to follow.

(You can record the lemon exercise and play it back yourself, or log on to MindOverBusiness.com for a free audio download of this exercise.)

Priming Yourself for Peak Performance

Perhaps the most powerful use of imagery prepares you for the tasks needed for success. It can be used to improve your performance in virtually any business situation.

Try this next exercise as another stepping stone to your goal.

EXERCISE

REFINING THE PICTURE

Find a comfortable place and close your eyes. Take a deep breath and hold it. Exhale strongly, and then breathe easily through the nose, feeling it in the back of your throat, then gently in the belly.

Picture yourself perfectly performing the skill that needs improvement. Imagine everything possible to the smallest detail. If you're a salesperson, see yourself giving a better close—the perfect close. See yourself sitting at the table, handing a client the pen as you say the right things in the right way that gets that person to sign the big deal. Notice your breathing, your physical presence, confidence, even your facial expression. Hear the sounds around you, a pen gliding across the contract. Feel yourself receiving the pen and the signed contract back from the client. Become aware of your feelings of pride and excitement with your sale. Listen to what you're saying to yourself and experience the feelings of success as if they are happening.

Let's take this exercise to the next step.

There are five slider controls in front of you. They will help you adjust and improve your visualization experience. Reach for the first control and slide it to adjust your internal zoom lens, making the image that you just practiced appear larger. Allow it to completely cover your mind screen, make it three-dimensional and vivid. Find the right zoom setting. How big must that image be to be at its most compelling? Now reach for a second control. As you slide it, enhance the colors in your mind's-eye screen. If it's black-and-white, colorize it. If it's already in color, make it more vivid, adding a "wow!" factor to it. With the third slider add brightness, make the picture more brilliant—or slide it down a little if it's too bright. Next, turn up the volume. Notice what happens when you make it loud, real loud—then the opposite: quiet. Notice the difference. Make the images just right. Finally, replay these images over and over. Study them, absorb and enjoy them. Continue to fine-tune the adjustments to keep your drive going strong.

Your personal power comes from making these images as clear, detailed and vivid as you can. Use all of your senses, applying everything at your disposal to make your visualizations as real and compelling as possible.

If you're working on images related to giving a presentation at a board meeting, make sure you imagine all the details: the color of the table, the placement of the chairs, the look of the whiteboard, the smell of the dry erase pens, the pouring of water from stainless steel pitchers into clear glasses, the sound of the laughter, the eyes riveted on you, your skillful handling of questions or objections, the applause at your conclusion, your exit from the meeting room with positive conclusions. Don't leave anything out. Sharpen and refine your imagery.

It's like the boxer who practices his skills by shadowboxing. He is making it as real as possible, so when he enters the real ring—or a businessperson enters a corporate boardroom—he goes on automatic pilot. It's as if he is already done. The brain is in peak condition to give the body and mouth the right things to do and say. The clearer the boxer's visualizations, the more precisely his self-talk heightens the imagery, making it more and more real, always leading to a better result.

Self-talk is real, and people often don't even realize that what they're thinking is having a negative impact on their performance. But they do it all the time. It's the baseball player at the plate thinking, "I hope he doesn't throw me an outside curve." And the next thing he knows, there's the outside curve and he misses it because he worried about it.

Improving Your Visualization Skills

The word "visualization" suggests that sight is the only sense used in this process. Not true.

You've already experienced how other senses are just as important in this performance-enhancing technique. As you practice imagery, you need to concentrate on using *all* of your senses in order to experience the moment fully as if it were really happening. If you're having difficulty keeping your images vivid, use those five sliders from the previous exercise to control your images. They influence brightness, size, color, volume and tone of voice, and the intensity of your feelings.

Go back to the Future Pace exercise (page 100) and take a few moments to recapture the image that you created about your success at some point in the future. In your mind's eye, take control of the slider. If you're struggling with confidence, imagine yourself in a situation in the past that made you uncomfortable. Imagine yourself now, in that same situation. What would you look like? How much more confident will you be? How would you stand? What kind of expression would be on your face? Feel how your clothes fit when you're confident. Feel your handshake when you're in control of yourself. Hear the sound of your conversation. Reach out and pick up an hors d'oeuvre at the company meeting as though you belong. Taste a canapé. Hear other people ask, "Who was that? She seemed so confident!"

Some of this may sound silly and trivial, but the more your mind can experience and anticipate, the better your chance at success. Imagery gives your mind a track to follow.

It's important that you use all of your senses and increase the intensity of your visualizations. The more involved you are, the more complete the pictures in your mind will be, allowing you to fully experience them as if they were really happening to you in the present.

As you practice your personal visualizations in the coming days and weeks, notice whether your visualizations are associated or dissociated. Are you fully engaged in your mind's movie, immersed with all of your senses as if you're truly in the action? That's associated visualization.

Or are you seeing the movie as if you're watching it as an observer? Dissociated visualizing has value as a learning tool for studying the nuances of preferred activity. For instance, if you're working on improving your assertiveness with your fellow managers, a dissociated image can help you see what you look like interacting with them today, and you can evaluate your results. It's as if you're an observer standing off on the sidelines watching yourself work. Once you've seen yourself interact, you can see a better way and step back into the picture as though it's happening now. Feel the right facial expressions and body posture, hear the choice of assertive words that allows you to be heard and respected among your peers. As your imagery becomes stronger, your body and mind will work together in harmony and, on a deep, micromuscular level, movements are then mimicked that will happen in real life.

Let's say, for example, that you have to give an important presentation and you really don't like public speaking. At the same time, it's something you want to do well. Ask yourself, "How far away am I from that goal?" To help answer this question, use dissociated visualization to clearly see where you are.

Next, switch your visualization to an associated state and imagine you have learned to do the presentation perfectly. The pictures in your mind should concentrate on what it would look like, feel like, sound like, smell like and taste like to make a beautiful presentation that results in thunderous applause and a happy audience. Take the actions that are spelled out in your visualization.

One of the biggest mistakes people often make in teaching visualization is that they don't know the difference between the associated state (as if doing it now/ownership) and dissociated state (watching yourself from afar). In fact, they never bother to distinguish between the two. As a result, many visualizers see their images as if they're happening to someone else. They even see themselves sitting on the sidelines watching themselves perform, and visualization never becomes the life-changing tool it could be.

MAKE IT A POSITIVE PICTURE

Throughout visualization, keep your images positive.

Picture yourself writing a great report (not one that's questioned and returned for a series of rewrites). See yourself making a perfect first call, choosing all the right words and language that match the tonality of your prospective client (not stumbling and mumbling as the person says, "Not interested!").

The images you visualize in this fashion are more likely to come true, so make sure these pictures are the ones you want to become part of your reality, including the skill levels you want to achieve.

Many great athletes have experienced the enormous power of a mental image that they've created. In the 2010 Winter Olympics in Vancouver, USA bobsled team driver and my client Steven Holcomb was disturbed by the sudden death of luger Nodar Kumaritashvili during a run on the same track he'd be hurdling down in just a few days. So Steve and I worked on a mental image of success and rephrased the language that commentators and other athletes were using to describe the run. They were saying things like it was "dangerous," and we changed that to "exciting." "Too fast" became "perfect opportunity." The dreaded, deadly 50-50 turn—Holcomb called it that in the media because he figured athletes had only a 50 percent chance of surviving it—morphed to "my advantage," which caused completely different imagery and led, in part, to the first USA gold medal in sixty-two years. I worked with the team until the day before the event.

TROUBLESHOOTING VISUALIZATION CHALLENGES

Sometimes I hear people say that they've tried visualization and it doesn't work.

They claim they don't have the patience for it or they lack the creativity or imagination to make it work. The truth is, *everyone* can visualize and improve performance through visualization. Some people simply have more trouble than others getting the process started.

If you have difficulty seeing images, focus more on the sounds and your internal dialogue. If you have difficulty with sounds, focus on the feelings, smells and tastes. Often using another modality will trigger the images in high definition as if you're performing perfectly. When things are fuzzy or vague, muted or dull, this may keep you from fully activating the neural pathways between mind and body and experiencing the ownership or micromuscular movements that can translate to improved performance in the business world.

If you are facing challenges with clear imagery, ask yourself questions such as these: What have my positive experiences of the past sounded like? How did I talk to myself? What did I hear around me? How did I feel? What did I touch? What did I smell or taste?

As you commit to the process of visualizing, don't be overly concerned about clarity and detail. Just getting a sense of it can cause change. Clarity will develop over time as your skills sharpen through repetition.

Most people think that visualization involves only the visual sense, but you really need the participation of all your senses for this technique to work. And visualization—like any skill worth developing—takes practice, so even if you're having difficulty at first, don't give up.

A good exercise to practice is to pick out an object in a room, study it, then close your eyes and try to see it again. Repeat this and you'll see more and more. Next, try projecting the image with your eyes open as well. Everything we do in business for the most part, we do with our eyes open. Just getting a sense of our success can send powerful signals to the brain. It's not as hard as it sounds; we daydream with our eyes open all the time. It doesn't block out what is going on consciously (most of the time, that is—don't do it while driving or operating heavy machinery, please!); it's a next-level skill to consciously project with your eyes open.

One of the first things I do with athletes is guide them to visualize in precise detail the equipment they use for their sport. For instance, a volleyball player will hold a volleyball in his hands, study it, close his eyes and tell me how many panels are on the ball. I have him open his eyes and study it again and then tell me where the inflation valve is. Or, what does the writing on the ball say? I want the player to notice how the ball feels in his hands and then set it aside and try to feel it as if it is still in his hands. He can hear the sounds the ball makes when it's served or passed. Working with these images and feelings makes the player sharper. We then expand from the ball to the entire volleyball court and develop images of him fully involved in the game: passing, serving, hitting, blocking, and playing defense.

Your use of visualizations can't be halfhearted or insincere. It needs to become a standard part of your business life. Just as a basketball player needs to practice physically shooting hundreds of balls a day, the player should also practice visual shooting on a daily basis.

To be a top salesperson you may need to make a certain number of new contacts every day and close at a certain ratio. Improve your odds of success by seeing all contacts expertly made and the sales that go with it. To get the most out of your visualization sessions, keep these guidelines in mind:

- **Finish Before You Start.** Know exactly what you want to accomplish before you begin. In your visualization, allow yourself to feel as though you've already achieved your goal.
- **Keep your imagery personal**, positive, detailed and in the present.
- **Experience all the emotions and feelings** that you possibly can. Whenever possible, keep all the images associated—that is, as if they're happening to you.
- **Don't force it.** Your subconscious may introduce dissociated images. That's okay! They have value. You should practice visualization, but don't worry about doing it perfectly. Let go and let your mind and body do their thing. If you think you see it, you do.
- **It's not magic.** Don't expect instant results, although there will be quick rewards for some people. Perform visualization a minimum of once in the morning and once at night. Be patient and your skills will improve.
- **Don't expect visualization to compensate** for a lackadaisical approach to acquiring the business and personal skills you need for success. You will need massive drive to get the job done.
- **Run through your visualization exercise** before an important event, reviewing what you want to accomplish. There is no denying that visualization can have a dramatic impact on your performance and your paycheck.

Cassie was the owner of a telemarketing firm in Omaha, Nebraska. She was struggling, looking for an edge, when she attended one of my public seminars. She needed the Mental Edge. As a female minority business owner, she never wanted to use race as a reason for success or failure. However, during tough times, or when contracts were lost to male-dominated companies, she would find herself wondering, "Was it the color of my skin?" "Is it because I am a woman?"

I taught her a new way to see herself, because if she went looking for excuses in an –ism, she could always find one. Who couldn't? We changed her paradigm, and she soon realized that women ran some of Omaha's best telemarketing firms. There were many successful minority-owned businesses in Omaha as well. I had her take inspiration from their success and visualize herself as the most qualified, most driven, most resilient person she could be.

Cassie learned to see herself as never letting rejection change her actions and that getting a no just meant she needed to get better and move that much closer to a yes. She began to see that being a woman gave her an edge because she would be perceived as more honest and less greedy than a man, and that being black made her stand out more, giving her the opportunity to be remembered more easily. It didn't matter if it was 100 percent true or not; life is a mind game, and you make the rules. And that became an effective rule for Cassie. She stood with the pride of a champion, heard the voice of her growing confidence, saw people liking her for who she was and . . . made up her mind that she was a winner regardless of a daily result or the views and opinions of others.

Her life changed overnight. Her business almost doubled in a year, and just as importantly, she enjoyed the process of success.

|||||||||||||||||||||||||||||||||| **E X E R C I S E** ||||||||||||||||||||||||||||||||||||||
A VISUALIZATION WORKOUT
||||||||||||||||||||||||||||||||||||||||||||||||||||||||||||||||||||||||||||||||||||||||||||||||||

As you practice visualization, use the worksheet below to keep track of how you're doing. I suggest writing down these items after your first visualization session and then about every two weeks thereafter as you continue to practice the technique.

WORKSHEET

My visualization goals are _____

_____

When I practice visualization, my experience is _____

_____

I do well in the following area(s): _____

_____

I can improve in the following area(s): _____

_____

My business performance is changing in the following ways: _____

_____

_____

||||||||||||||||||||||||||||||||||||||||||||||||||||||||||||||||||||||||||||||||||||||||||||||||||

Self-Talk

By combining visualization with proper self-talk, you will increase your chances of success.

Some people are much more auditory than visual, and the auditory input really moves them. At other times, people that are highly auditory access more visual parts of their brains by well-chosen Performance Talk.

Performance Talk is much more than mindless chatter or positive thinking. It directs the mind to access, find and/or learn needed skills for success. This type of internal dialogue creates imagery and emotion leading to action. If there is no resultant action, what's the point? Many people manage to feel good even though they're going nowhere.

The challenge for many people is that their internal dialogue is cluttered and filled with self-doubt and negativity:

- "I can't learn this new job, I'm too old!"
- "I never stick to my goals."
- "I am not smart enough."

If these are the kinds of statements you're repeating to yourself, what do you think is going to happen? Of *course* you're not going to perform at your peak! We all talk to ourselves throughout the day— mostly quietly, some mumbling to themselves, others loud enough to be heard clearly—reacting to challenges and opportunities as they arise. The statements we make are based on information we gather and filter through our belief system, and they become our reality even if they are not based on fact. Self-talk based on this information can limit our performance and make us feel really bad and inadequate, with a "Why even try?" attitude.

When our internal chatter is filled with negative criticism, when it reminds us of our limitations and failings, it can ruin our focus, undermine our confidence and make it harder to perform.

Performance Talk, on the other hand, is a technique for sending positive messages to your brain and body. It is a step beyond positive thinking, as it gives your mind a course of action while surrounding you in a mental environment of excellence that supports your action plan and goals. The skillful use of the right words can condition your mind to focus on your strengths, not your limitations. It is extremely useful in changing an unwanted habit or learning a new skill.

Performance Talk is quality thinking. It has a ripple effect, influencing and displacing other thoughts. Imagine a smooth, glassy lake that is still and quiet. Throw a small stone in the center of the lake and that small stone impacts the entire placid body of water, as circular waves radiate from the small rock's influence, from shoreline to shoreline.

A positive or negative thought has the same impact on your mind and body as the stone. One thought affects the whole, and since your thoughts are a choice, choose Performance Talk and send out positive wave after positive wave. This technique has the ability to transform you as a person, to shake up old, limiting belief systems and propel you in a new direction.

The most important thing about Performance Talk is that it needs to be *action*-oriented as opposed to just a parroting of the wealth of positive motivation attitude statements that are out there, such as "Think big," or "Go hard or go home." What does that even *mean*?

Performance Talk is:

- "I sell effectively *because* I make a hundred cold calls a day."
- "I'm a 90 percent free-throw shooter *because* I follow through."

The "because" is based on something you're not doing that you know you need to do. Performance Talk leads to a specific action, and your brain will see that action and strive to duplicate that consistently.

"I'm a great salesperson *because* I create rapport." Are you going to get rapport just telling yourself, "I'm a great salesperson, I'm a great salesperson, I'm a great salesperson"? Where's the action in that?

A lot of motivational speakers will tell you, "Just see the big picture." But you have to see the details. The world looks quite different across a desk than it does from thirty thousand feet up. Which venue are you likely to be performing in next?

|||||||||||||||||||||||||||||||||||||||||||||| **E X E R C I S E** ||||||||||||||||||||||||||||||||||||||||||||||

PERFORMANCE TALK

||||||||||||||||||||||||||||||||||||||||||||||||||||||||||||||||||||||||||||||||||||||||||||||||||||||||

1. Determine something in your personal or business life that you want to change. It may be a characteristic, behavior or skill level.

2. Use the space below to write out an "I am" statement that describes your goal as already accomplished. For example, a salesperson might say, "I am a great salesperson," even though her closing skills are weak. A shy person might say, "I am outgoing," even when he is a work in progress. A slow typist might say, "I am a fast typist," even though she is currently typing sixty words per minute.

I am: _____

3. Refine your statement by making it more specific and attaching emotion to it. To reshape your statement, ask questions like, "How much more do I want to sell?" "How outgoing do I need to be?" "How many words do I want to type?" The result might look like this:

I am a great salesperson because I am always closing.

I am outgoing and assertive, initiating greetings and conversation.

I am a fast typist because I remove distractions and I focus.

Performance Talk needs to be realistic. It shouldn't place an extra burden on you, nor should it be so unbelievable or improbable that your mind can't effectively use it. For example, "I am a great soccer player because I score every time I kick the ball" could be instead "I am a great soccer player because I *am ready to score at any time.*"

The value of Performance Talk is unparalleled. Use it daily to change your performance now. When you wake up in the morning, repeat your Performance Talk out loud, with power and belief. At night, before you go to bed, gently repeat and imagine your Performance Talk and let it be the last thing you "see" before going to sleep, as your brain is particularly receptive at this time.

Archie was a painter who was always out of work. He was extremely laid back, a super-nice guy who did good work, but he didn't like to sell himself or his talents.

After seeing painter after painter doing shoddy work but making lots of money, he decided to do something about his situation and enrolled in my Mental Edge training program. He had heard about visualizing as a high school baseball player, but it really didn't work for him. He gave it a try with me, but honestly, there was no magic spark . . . until he paired visualization with Performance Talk.

Previously, the images he saw were always knocked out by a subtle negative loop passed on from his dad: "If you do good work, people will find you. You don't need to sell." Archie was stuck on this wishful fantasy that his well-intentioned father had passed on to him.

Together we constructed a more effective loop that was just as much fantasy as what his dad gave to him. It was simple and straightforward: "I do good work and people deserve my work. I am valuable and worthy and always prospecting. To reach people, I *must* prospect." He realized that for more people to receive his value he would have to sell more, and do it for their own good!

Archie didn't just say it. He believed it, he felt it, and he wrote it on an index card and taped it to his mirror. Every morning, he read it out loud with passion. Then it was easy to see the corresponding images of action. His internal dialogue became "I must sell. I must prospect." He went from being this guy who waited around for people to find him to one who went out and found *them*. Archie's Performance Talk became "I am valuable and worthy and love to prospect." He talked to people at gas stations, grocery stores— wherever opportunity struck, he presented a business card. His income increased 43 percent the next year and continued to grow for the next seven years, until he retired.

Performance Talk is a way of affirming that you can perform at the level of your Desire Statement. There is nothing more powerful than a made-up mind, and Performance Talk will help you to make up your mind, learn new skills quicker and change behavior fast.

One of the keys to effective Performance Talk is to feel what it is you're saying. If your Performance Talk is personal, positive, emotional and in the present, it will reinforce your resolve to do what needs to be done for success.

6

Pyramids Are Just a Bunch of Blocks

We all have some of the building blocks of success and can gain access to the others. The trick is to assemble them in the right order.

We need the proper foundation, and it must get stronger. The bigger and better the foundation, the taller your pyramid will stand. We must have strength at the bottom so we can build our own pyramid of success.

If you don't put the blocks in the right order, if you lack the proper foundation, sooner or later the structure will collapse all around—and maybe on top of—you. It's the way a life is constructed that makes it something special.

In this chapter, I emphasize that you can't just wake up in the morning with a big grin on your face and go conquer the world. There is an order to the way we create ourselves to reach our goals and new heights every day.

The Great Pyramid of Giza was 480.69 feet tall,* and, for 3,800 years, it was the tallest man-made structure in the world. Each side was 755.76 feet long. The base was horizontal and flat, and the corners were set at almost perfect angles. This precise foundation determined how high the Great Pyramid could be built. The foundation allowed this oldest of the Seven Wonders of the Ancient World to remain standing tall to this day.

You can only go as high as the foundation you build. The builders of the Great Pyramid of Giza knew this and, with painstaking accuracy, set their foundation. They didn't always have the building materials they needed at hand, so they often went hundreds of miles under great hardship to get what they deemed necessary to succeed. They couldn't do the job if they didn't invent new ways of building and stay focused on a perfect foundation, or if they merely maintained the 2560 BC status quo.

The building blocks of success must be acquired before they can be assembled into anything. You don't have to be perfect; you just need the strongest possible foundation on which to build. Your foundation will be particular to your profession but will share common building blocks with others.

I vividly remember digging foundations for houses as a young man. I was the new guy, so while an operator ran a tractor with a digging scoop, I was on the ground with a standard shovel, cleaning the edges, leveling the depth. Backbreaking work, to say the least. The foundation was reinforced with rebar and then a denser concrete was poured—denser because it had to withstand the weight of a house and the unpredictable forces of the California earth.

My karate foundation is solid because I trained with the best.

---

* "Dimensions and Mathematics of the Great Pyramid," www.theglobaleducationproject.org/egypt/studyguide/gpmath.php.

Now I must continue to build on it as my students get better or they will end up better than me!

Your foundation must be able to support you through the changing world we live in, so you can sway with the movements of time but never break.

Attitude Is Everything

The main mental building block is attitude. Attitude is everything. It will allow you to do what needs to be done whether you want to do it or not. How do you get a great attitude? Attitudes are not floating in the air for you to reach out and grab. Attitudes are learned and reinforced by our environment, parents, friends, the music we listen to, the schools and churches we attend and many other things.

At the same time, it's easy to choose an attitude that makes us more effective. Most people never do this, as they let their attitude control them instead of them controlling their attitude. Every day we can make a choice: Is this a good day or a bad day? What makes it a good day? What makes it a bad day? You can choose to be a good student or a poor student. It has nothing to do with smart or dumb. You can choose to love the city you live in or be miserable there.

I hear people all the time lament their circumstances and do nothing to change them because of a defeatist attitude. It's common to hear intelligent adults whine and complain about their jobs, bosses and coworkers, not realizing they have the power to make their own lives better. It's simple: either find another job or change your attitude.

Here are some simple ways to generate a winning attitude:

- List the things you like about your job.
- List the things your job allows you to enjoy.
- List the things you like about your coworkers and all the things they have done for you.
- What are the things your boss does right?
- What do you appreciate about your boss?

You can also do this exercise by replacing "work" with school or any social group. Take all of the positives you've listed and relive them right now. Visualize the episodes on the list. Remember them with all the exciting detail, color and sound you recall, calling on all of your senses. Look at your job and where you are at right now and ask yourself, "What is the most important thing I have to be thankful for?" Visualize it, feel it, hear it, taste it, smell it—experience it in full detail.

Now how do you feel about your job?

From this moment forward, adopt an attitude that reflects this. Give coworkers the benefit of the doubt, appreciate your boss for what he or she can do and don't pick at what your boss can't do. Set your attitude in stone. "I will be thankful every day because I am healthy and have a job to go to." You are at work eight-plus hours a day. If you work for forty-five years, you will spend more than ninety thousand hours of your life at work. Ninety thousand hours! You can slough through it as just a job or make it an adventure.

Maybe it's not your dream job, but it's the one that pays your bills now. A better attitude will enhance your ability to ride out the tough days and position you for when a new opportunity comes around. And, in the meantime, it will keep you from being miserable and hungry *today*.

This primary building block of attitude will serve you well, regardless of your occupation, and will determine how high you rise.

Breathe . . . Relax . . . *Activate*

One of the foundation stones in your pyramid is to harness the power of breath. This simple action helps harmonize the mind and body and makes you more receptive to change.

Many people take the power of breathing for granted. After all, you've been breathing all your life, about 26,000 times a day, mostly without conscious thought. But just try holding your breath for six minutes and see what happens! Breathing is vital. Each breath is more important than food or water, yet rarely appreciated until it's your last one!

Proper breathing will relax the body, calm the mind and allow you to make the best choices in intense situations with petty coworkers, a subordinate screwup and the sometimes irate public. The belly breathing you will learn in this section will reduce stress, improve learning and clarify visualizations. You will learn to breathe, relax and activate the right resources at the right time.

One of the quickest ways to gain control of emotions and thoughts is by belly breathing, as it oxygenates the blood more thoroughly in the lower lobes of the lungs. Oxygen-rich blood revitalizes all the cells in the body, including the brain cells that encourage clear thinking. In my experience as a trainer of professional and amateur athletes, it's also been a huge benefit for increased endurance, strength and recovery. We enhance a highly trained athlete's strength by 3 percent on average and routinely improve an untrained athlete's strength by as much as 10 percent just by teaching proper breathing.

Take a moment now to pay attention to your breath.

EXERCISE
HOW DO YOU BREATHE?

Lightly place one hand on your upper chest. Put your thumb and your forefinger gently along your collarbone. Place your other hand lightly on your belly with your thumb around your navel area and just breathe normally ten times.

Where did you feel the most movement? In your belly or your chest? Most people tend to breathe improperly, with too much upper chest movement. These thoracic breathers take shallow, choppy breaths, thus creating a buildup of carbon dioxide in the bloodstream, impairing their concentration, clouding their thinking and causing undue stress. Oftentimes it's the stress of the business that keeps them unconsciously breathing this way, compounding the stress in a vicious circle. This is the wrong way to breathe if your goal is to maximize your potential. You need to learn to breathe deeper in the lungs, what's called diaphragmatic or belly breathing (the diaphragm is a thin membrane separating the abdominal area and the lungs).

The diaphragm and the belly don't actually breathe. We use the terms metaphorically to allow you to sink the air you breathe deeply into the lungs. When I train athletes and get them into a relaxed state, I tell them to breathe *normally*, through the nose, back of the throat and gently in the belly, as the belly rises and falls and the chest is still. The idea is to link your understanding of "normal" to this way of breathing. You need to do it as well. Take gentle, gradual, deep breaths, filling up your entire lungs, beginning with the lowest areas and working your way up. Once you make use of the lungs in their entirety and oxygenate the blood more thoroughly, you will begin to use your lower lungs more efficiently. Like any new skill, this takes practice and is a vital block in your foundation of success.

When you think of diaphragmatic breathing, think of watching a baby sleep. The baby breathes deeply and rhythmically from the belly, no worries and no fear. A baby breathes naturally. My son adopted a puppy, and when you watch the little one sleep, she has no worry, no fear; she just breathes, and that little belly rises and falls.

As a businessperson, you can't just walk around the office so relaxed and calm from deep belly breathing that you don't want to work. That's counterproductive; your breathing must lead to proper action.

Notice a lion hunting in a typical Discovery Channel nature documentary. Even as it stalks its prey, its breathing is deep and rhythmic, cool and controlled. When the time is right to pounce, the proper natural actions are triggered as the lion explodes from the bushes to bring down an antelope. Even under the stress of hunting, the lion breathes naturally, deeply and rhythmically, from the belly. No worries, no fear, just hunt. It's not thinking of failure; it's conditioned for success.

Consider that lion. It's not thinking, "What if I *miss* the antelope?" It's not looking around, worried that someone is going to judge its hunting prowess. You need to become more like the lion. And you will when you use belly breathing to harmonize the mind and body, reducing stress, increasing mental clarity and calming the nerves and emotions so you can use all your energy for the right actions at the right time.

Do this next exercise to harness the power of proper breathing.

||||||||||||||||||||||||||||||||||||||||||||||||||||||||||||||||||||||||||||||||||||||||||||||||||||||||||||||||||||||||||||||||||||||||||

|||||||||||||||||||||||||||||||||||||||||||||| **E X E R C I S E** ||||||||||||||||||||||||||||||||||||||||||||||
PROPER BREATHING
||||||||||||||||||||||||||||||||||||||||||||||||||||||||||||||||||||||||||||||||||||||||||||||||||||||||||||||||||||||||||||||||||||||||||

Place one hand lightly on your upper chest and the other on your belly. Gently take a breath through your nose, down the back of the throat, inhaling deep into your lower lungs. Allow your belly to effortlessly expand as you progressively fill your lungs with air from bottom to top. Make sure only the hand on your belly moves. Keep your chest still. Hold the breath at the bottom for two to three seconds, then slowly exhale through the nose and the mouth. Feel your belly contract as you do. Exhale all the air. Take a little longer to exhale than you did to inhale. Pause before the next breath. Continue to breathe slowly. With each breath, your belly should rise as you inhale and contract as you exhale. Do this for a total of ten breaths. Experience your breathing naturally shift lower and feel more relaxation with each breath.

When I teach martial arts, one of the first techniques I teach my students is to control their breathing and stay in control of their emotions so they can take the right action at the right time. Proper breathing helps them synchronize the mind (both the right and left hemispheres) with the body so that they become one with what they are trying to accomplish.

I once trained a high school tennis player who went on to become Orange County Player of the Year and to play at Princeton University. It was evident at our first session that his breathing was high and shallow in any stressful situation. He would worry about making his second serve, and his breath and his actions would betray him. If he questioned how to return serve, his breath would go shallow and he would tighten up. I taught him how to control his breathing so that when that happened, he could relax quickly and naturally and take the right action at the right time. He learned to take natural, deep breaths during potentially stressful situations, and his results improved immediately.

You can use this tool right now. Before your next presentation, performance review or interaction with an upset consumer, breathe naturally, deep in the belly, three times before you speak. Before your next audit, creative graphic arts project or brainstorming meeting, take three belly breaths before you start writing or creating and let the thoughts flow. People who are out of control with anger breathe high and shallow, which causes more tension and anxiety, making things worse. But rhythmic diaphragmatic breathing has a calming, soothing effect and gives you a better chance of taking the right action at the right time.

It's not uncommon to find belly breathing a challenge. An exercise I created to speed up your learning curve is simple and effective.

SPEED UP YOUR LEARNING CURVE
|||||||||||||||||||||||||||||||||||||||||||||||||||||||||||||||||||||||||||||||||||||||||||||||||||||||||||

Lie down someplace comfortable. Make sure there are no distractions for the next three to five minutes. Take a book with some weight to it, like a hardcover, or a small 2.5-pound weight (which is what I use with athletes). Put the center of the book or weight over your navel, close your eyes and breathe normally and gently through your nose, back of your throat, and deeply in the belly. Keeping your chest still, focus on gently raising the weight without holding your breath. Do this effortlessly for three to five minutes, once a day, for the next three days. That should be enough to create this learning in your body. You can go longer if need be.

INSTANT RELAXATION TECHNIQUE (IRT)

This is a good time to introduce an effective technique that can have a major impact for you right now.

The IRT will allow you to feel changes in your body and mind as you are able to change your state and relax on cue. I first used this technique in 1983 to relax basketball players with remarkable success just before free throws. Basketball is often played at a frantic pace, and it's a game of reaction. When a foul is made, the game comes to a halt and a player goes from sprinting up and down the court to having ten seconds to shoot a free throw. The player goes from a ballistic reactive activity to a static mechanical movement. This ten-second gap between thought and action allows all types of negative thoughts and mechanical breakdowns to occur. The IRT fills in the gap with relaxed breathing and clear directional thoughts leading to perfect posture and mechanics and a zone-like mindlessness causing right action at the right time.

IRT can work for you as a de-stresser in traffic or to clear your mind before a test. It can be used to relax and free the mind to find the right words or creativity before a sales call or brainstorming session.

▏▏▏▏▏▏▏▏▏▏▏▏▏▏▏▏▏▏▏▏▏▏▏▏ E X E R C I S E ▏▏▏▏▏▏▏▏▏▏▏▏▏▏▏▏▏▏▏▏▏▏▏▏
INSTANT RELAXATION TECHNIQUE

1. Gently and slowly take a deep breath, filling up the lungs from bottom to top. Exhale forcefully.

2. Breathe normally for a few breaths.

3. Gently take another deep breath, filling the lungs fully as you simultaneously make a fist with your nondominant hand. Hold the breath and the fist (tight but not too tight) for about three seconds, then exhale slowly and release the fist simultaneously.

Breathe normally as your forehead goes smooth, your eyes are soft, your cheeks are loose, and your jaw is slack. Your lips are slightly separated, your neck is free, and your shoulders are down as you allow your chest to go still while your belly rises and falls.

4. Imagine your relaxation place. It can be anywhere: mountains, beach, desert, the house in which you grew up. Experience it as if you are there now. What do you see? Hear? Smell? Taste? Feel? Notice what you say to yourself when you are there. Notice the tone of your voice. Become aware of the colors you see. What color is the most dominant? What do you hear around you? How are you breathing? Take note of your posture. What do you feel like when you are totally relaxed, with no worries, no fears? What's a word that describes how you feel when you are relaxed at this place? Notice the word in the palm of your nondominant hand. Notice the font or style of the letters. What color is your word? Gently take a deep breath, make a firm fist and hold your breath and the fist for three seconds. Gently exhale and, as you do, open your fist at the same time. After a few seconds, see your colored word in the palm of your hand as you gently say your word and simultaneously touch your thumb and your forefinger (or one of your other fingers) for just a second, release and breathe as a newborn baby, no worries, no fears, life is good.

(You can record these instructions and play them back, or log on to my website, MindOverBusiness.com, for a free IRT audio download.)

This process needs to be done every day over the next seven days. Do it more than once a day if you like. Everyone is different, but sometime between your first seven sessions, you will successfully install the desired response of relaxation every time you do the stimulus, touch thumb and finger, and say your word.

My use of this cue has been helpful in so many ways, including the first business workshop I ever conducted in Manhattan. I was coming from the Midwest and had heard that New York crowds were tough. I was intimidated. I was all of twenty-seven years old, and many people in the audience were older and more successful than me. I wasn't five minutes into my presentation when a woman stood up from her seat and abruptly and angrily challenged me on something I said. My mind went momentarily blank. Then I gently squeezed my wrist—my cue—without anyone knowing what I was doing. I don't know what I said, but the words flowed, and the woman thanked me and sat down. Six hours later, when the session was over, she stood up again and started a standing ovation! I was on automatic pilot and touched down perfectly.

PERFORMANCE CUES

The IRT you just used is a skillful application of performance cues, a stimulus that elicits a predictable response.

One of the most famous and oft-referenced stimulus/response studies ever conducted was by the Russian psychophysiologist Ivan Pavlov (1849–1936).* Pavlov's research into the workings of the digestive system eventually led him to develop the science of conditioned reflexes.

His 1903 paper, "The Experimental Psychology and Psychopathology of Animals," led Pavlov to win the Nobel Prize in Physiology or Medicine in 1904. His now-famous experiment with dogs best illustrated the conditioning process. Pavlov would ring a bell while showing a hungry dog some meat, and the dog would salivate in anticipation of eating it. After repeating this process many times, Pavlov eliminated the middle step—that is, he rang the bell but didn't show the meat to the dog. But because of the repeated pairing of the bell and the meat, the dog had become conditioned to salivate whenever he heard the bell. The bell became a cue, or a sensory stimulus, that the dog responded to in a consistent way.

As humans, we're constantly conditioned by the linking of stim-

---

* "The Nobel Prize in Physiology or Medicine 1904: Ivan Pavlov," http://nobelprize.org/nobel_prizes/medicine/laureates/1904/pavlov-bio.html.

ulus and response, and it's typically outside of our control. For example, if we're driving down the street thinking that we're obeying the law, when we look in our rearview mirror and there are flashing red lights, we immediately respond to the stimulus. We may say a few choice words, but we clench the steering wheel, our chest gets tight, and we start thinking of excuses.

Advertisers know the power of a stimulus and response and turn up the volume of their television commercials to pound in the auditory cues. Commercials are bright and flashy to condition visual cues. Advertisers simulate taste and smell and good feelings to get you to buy their cheeseburger.

Cues give permanence to an experience. They reinforce certain feelings and emotions within us even though we're not consciously responding to the cues. For instance, a song from the past comes on the radio—"Sugar Sugar" by the Archies. It may take us back to a moment in time that we remember vividly, hearing it for the first time on a school bus, even though it was decades ago. We may have a flood of memories with emotions—the pretty girl in the miniskirt sitting across the aisle at the time or just the potholes in the road—that can bring a smile or a tear to our eye.

In the same way, Dean Starkey, a world-class pole-vaulter, would smell newly mowed grass and instantly replay his first nineteen-foot pole vault in Brazil. I actually created this performance cue for him. It thrust him into his Maximum Performance State (MPS), helping him vault nineteen feet five times the following season.

And even when performance cues happen inadvertently, they can still cause a lasting response. A budding chef who burns dinner for the first time—setting off the smoke detector—will become panicky every time the kitchen starts to heat up, fearing the return of the piercing sound. Others in the family use it as a signal that dinner is ready!

To help you get into the proper performance state at the proper time, performance cues need to be created by you. You need to create words, feelings, smells and tastes that reinforce actions you want to take.

Chris Mabeus, who was drafted by the Oakland A's in 2001, learned to relax between pitches by associating the way he hit his glove on his thigh with relaxation. Every time he would get into a relaxed state he would touch his thigh with his glove a certain way, and after repeated conditioning, his body began to interpret that particular touch on the thigh as a cue to relax.

I once gave six all-day seminars in six days, and the night before the first one began, I came down with a sore throat and major cold. My voice became a gravelly whisper, and I stayed up late into the night visiting the sauna, drinking hot tea with lemon, and sucking on throat lozenges trying to get my voice back. But it was to no avail. I woke up sick and tired, with a voice that was barely audible. I had a performance cue that I had been using for years while playing sports. I used this cue to put me in a peak performance state, turned up the microphone, and proceeded as if I felt wonderful. I got through the day, jumped on an airplane and flew from Denver to Austin. I checked into my room in Austin, crashed as soon as I hit the bed, woke up a few hours later and did it all over again. I did this for four of the six seminars, and by the fifth one, I felt like myself again. My cue was simple. I replayed all of my past successes as an athlete and all the challenges I successfully overcame in business, got the feelings, the sights and sounds that went with them, put them all into my right hand, made a fist and said with passion and belief, "Yes!" That became my cue.

Performance cues often become rituals, and you will see this as athletes perform.

One of my favorite baseball players as a kid was Cincinnati Reds second baseman and Hall of Famer Joe Morgan. As a batter, he would flap one arm in a unique way between pitches. He had to do this to hit the ball.

Boston Red Sox first baseman Kevin Youkilis has perhaps the most unique performance cue in all of baseball. When he comes to bat, he swivels his hips like a pole dancer, simultaneously raises his bat high above his head and swings it around in a continuous circular motion. A lot of fans think it's the silliest thing they've ever seen, but it works for Youkilis, who has a career batting average of .294 and a World Series ring to show for it. Youkilis is successful, so he can use his natural cue and tie it to success. By contrast, a .200 hitter might want to keep searching for a better cue.

NBA star and Naismith Memorial Basketball Hall of Famer Michael Jordan possessed one of the most famous performance cues of all time as he would glide through the air with his tongue sticking out. It elicited the response of an incredible athletic performance.

To create your own personal, unique performance cue, you want to pick a word and/or a physical reminder that is easy to replay as needed. A cue can be used to help you relax or to activate all the resources you need for success.

Creating the reminder is easy. Just pick a physical action and tie it to the visualization and feeling of a desired performance. The cue can be totally random, something that simply reminds you and you alone, but use a cue that is not something you do all the time. For example, if you always tug on your left ear out of habit, don't make that a performance cue, because there is already a habit tied to that. It has to be something you consciously choose that's easy to do and duplicates consistently. You don't want to touch your pointer finger knuckle one time, your middle finger knuckle the second time, and your fingernail the third time. You need to repeat the same cue and keep stacking successes onto it. I squeeze my wrist in a certain way before I go on stage. I've tied all my visualizations of relaxed, successful speaking engagements to the cue, and I do it before I go up on the platform, but I chose it by design. A cue has to be something that, when you are comfortable with it, doesn't draw attention to you. The key is to make the cue easy to repeat and replay in the same exact way every time. It may be as simple as touching your thumb and forefinger together. It may be a grab of your wrist or a tug on your tie.

Don't use an inadvertent cue you may already be using, as it may be connected to negative feelings, imagery or results. Choose something that you can use in the natural course of your business day without drawing attention to yourself. You really don't want to stand in front of a boardroom and pat yourself on top of the head three times and spin around in a circle. Your message might get lost and your job security could be jeopardized.

Cue words take a little more work. They can be said internally or out loud. You will need to visualize and experience the state you want to be in and extract a word from that experience. Get the feeling as if it's happening now, and allow your mind to search for a word that describes the feeling, and let that be your performance cue. It can be any word unique to you, as standard as "energize," or something more colorful, like "yee-*haw*!" You may find the words that pop out are written in significant colors, fonts or styles of writing. Use these to make your words more significant and compelling.

Maybe you are too hyper and want to calm down and relax. If that's the issue, replay times in your life when you were relaxed and calm. See, feel, hear, smell and taste everything you can about your experiences, and when you feel totally relaxed, let your mind search out a word that describes how you feel. It can be anything, as basic as "calm" or "serene" or something esoteric and symbolic, like "clouds." This would then be the word you would use for your IRT.

These cues will help you to get more out of this book, as they condition your mind and body to be better than you have ever been. They will trigger positive emotions and actions as you learn to go on automatic pilot and soar to greater heights.

EXERCISE
SUCCESS HISTORY + PERFORMANCE CUES

Now let's do a Success History Search with Performance Cues and see what another mental building block can contribute.

Everybody has some type of success in his or her background. Everybody has a history that's made that person who he or she is. You might be the poor kid who grew up lower middle class, whose dad was never there and whose mom raised him, and you blame your failures on whiny stories that explain why you are where you are. Or you can see the same events in a *positive* way. In the movie *The Blind Side*, which is based on a true story, a homeless boy named Michael Oher overcomes a traumatic childhood and becomes an all-American college football player (and later, an NFL star). In the course of the film, he literally closes his eyes during the bad things in his life and focuses only on the good.

It's how *you* see your history that's important.

If you go through your history in the right frame of mind, you'll find multiple successes, from the time you first tied a shoe, to the first bike you rode, the first A+ on a term paper, to when you thought you couldn't do something and you did it anyway. Stack all those successes, and you will realize that you have more value than you probably give yourself credit for. Again, it's perspective. That's how we can see ourselves as having more resources than we once thought we did.

First, think of a physical cue that you can use before you have to perform. It can be as simple as pumping a fist or slapping your hands together. It can be more covert, like pulling on your right earlobe or squeezing the first knuckle of your middle finger. Don't worry about making the wrong choice as you go through these exercises; your own choices will evolve and become more efficient.

Now find a place to relax without interruptions. Sit back, close your eyes, breathe normally through your nose, the back of your throat and gently in the belly. After a few breaths, do your IRT and think about one of the most recent times when you were successful:

- What did you accomplish?

- Where were you?

- What were you wearing?

- What kind of expression did you have on your face?

- What did you say to yourself?

- What did it feel like when you knew you were successful?

Breathe in all the experiences of prior success. What word pops into your mind that describes this sensation? Now say your word with passion as you make your physical cue. Think of another time when you were happy with the results you achieved. How did you know you were successful? Notice the sounds around you. Listen to how you talk to yourself and become aware of the tone of your voice. What would it look like watching yourself succeed? How does it feel now owning the success?

Use the same word you used earlier to describe the feelings of success. Say the word with passion as you simultaneously make your physical cue.

Now it's time to remember a third success from when you were younger still. Remember where you were? Is there a sound or a song you associate with that success? Become aware of any smells or tastes of your success. Who do you share your feelings of victory with? How does it feel right now as you breathe in all the emotions?

Say your cue word with passion as you simultaneously make your physical cue and experience the posture and facial expressions of a winner. Hear the self-talk of a champion.

As a result of stacking cues, you may notice a deeper feeling or more real experience in the future. When a time comes that you need to perform, do your cue first and step into a better performance. You are now ready to begin using performance cues to impact your day-to-day business activity.

7

Focus and Concentration for Right Actions

Successful people do what needs to be done whether they want to or not. That is a huge difference between people who are successful and people who are not. They can focus and follow through on whatever is needed. You need to know what needs to be done on a practical level and then do it in order to be successful.

- What does your enterprise require?
- How many hours a day do you have to work?
- What do you have to get done?

Focus on those three factors. We live in a world of distractions, television, Internet and business meetings. You need to focus on what truly needs to be done. There's a bottom line in everybody's job. You need to know what that is in yours and get it accomplished daily.

You have now written a Desire Statement, set goals and enhanced your use of visualization and self-talk in order, and taking these steps has heightened your passion. But there is still more work to be done, more successful clues to be followed.

Patterns of Excellence Are All Around You

The best way to get a job done right is to follow a proven pattern. Think about McDonald's and other hugely successful franchises. A pattern of excellence cuts down on trial and error, and you can focus on doing the right thing at the right time because someone else has already shown you how. All around you are clues to the right way to do things. If you organize the clues, you get a pattern that will give you a repeatable success each and every time.

When I met Ben Clymer, he dreamed of one day running his own auto body shop instead of being an employee. Work ethic was not a problem for Ben, but knowing how to run a successful body shop business was.

I suggested he follow "Success Leaves Clues" (Perception Stretcher 7 in Chapter 4) as the best way to increase his chance of making good. Next he took a job with a highly profitable repair chain. Starting at the lowest rung, he banged out fenders but used his innate curiosity about and understanding of the business to move up into management. He studied the inner workings of the business—insurance billing, parts buying, estimating, customer service, hiring and retaining quality workers—all the while making extra money on the side by working on friends' cars at night and on weekends at home.

Ben eventually took charge of a number of the company's shops. He was a student of my Mental Edge program and today owns and operates three Ben Clymer Body Shops in Southern California and is living his dream.

Look at the clues other successful people have left behind, so that you can use their past successes and make it easier on yourself. Don't reinvent the wheel. And don't follow somebody who failed; follow somebody who succeeded.

WHAT ARE THE CLUES?

I compiled a list of the top attributes of successful businesspeople. These were people from all professions, including billionaires, those worth hundreds of millions of dollars and those who had successful businesses with incomes that allowed them to live their dreams. These were people with sustainable businesses that could be patterned effectively.

The list was then sent out to a group of forty-six successful businesspeople I knew (thirty-seven responded) to rank in order of importance. Here is my original list, and below it is the same list but with the top ten qualities ranked in order of importance by some of the most successful businesspeople in the world.

1. Knowledge
2. Business Plan
3. Money
4. Network
5. Goal Setting
6. Passion
7. Vision
8. Work Ethic
9. Communication Skills
10. Marketing

11. Awareness
12. Competitiveness
13. Positive Attitude
14. Confidence
15. Motivation
16. Self-Belief
17. Luck
18. Imagination

19. Integrity
20. Character
21. Courage
22. Self-Esteem
23. Drive
24. Focus
25. Flexibility

The value in studying the top ten rankings is that there are clear and obvious choices that, when applied to ambition, heighten our chance of success.

1. Passion
2. Vision
3. Imagination
4. Focus
5. Work Ethic

6. Competitiveness
7. Belief in Self, Dream
8. Specific Knowledge
9. Character
10. Luck

It was interesting that all the participants said that business plans are important but that they are worthless if the top ten aren't in place. Respondents also felt that if you had passion and vision, motivation would take care of itself and that work ethic trumps motivation.

The number one success clue is passion. We need passion! Passion is where drive and motivation come together to make us unstoppable. How do we get it? It goes back to our Desire Statement and our belief that we can make it come true. It's very difficult to get passionate about something we don't believe we can have.

Number two is vision: a clear direction and path to follow. It's the opposite of wishy-washy or "I *think* I *might* try this." It might be a clear career path like the one Eloise took. She made up her mind to be a radiologist and ultrasound tech, then took a job to work her way through school at a hospital where she wanted to work after she earned her degree. She picked a prestigious school with the fastest track and got it done. All of that earned her the resources to pursue her *real* passion: surfing and travel.

Billionaire Henry Samueli—who with his partner Henry Nicholas started Broadcom, global leader in semiconductors for wired and wireless communications—had a clear vision of how technology could impact the world. They didn't hope or wish. They had vision and the imagination to project future applications of their product. Their focus was laser-precise and their work ethic legendary, with an incredible degree of competitiveness. Nicolas, by the way, loved to push himself to the limit and test his physical abilities in the weight room. They earned formal educations— PhDs—and the specific knowledge of their industry. Sprinkled in was a little bit of luck, too, as they were in the right place at the right time.

EXERCISE
PASSION

If you were guaranteed to be successful, what business would you be in?

1st choice: _____

2nd choice: _____

3rd choice: _____

What would be your reward? _____

_____

What's the first step you can take to make this a reality?

I will _____

What resources do you need to make this happen?

I will acquire _____

Not ready to be on your own yet? Let's draw passion from your current job. What is the number one thing that still excites you about it?

_____

_____

How can you do more of that?

_____

What are your rewards?

_____

What else would you like to do with your current employer?

_____

How can you accomplish that?

_____

What's the first step to make this happen?

Focus on building individual blocks of success and arranging them in ways that most benefit you. You will be amazed how much fun your work becomes. Your productivity will skyrocket and your days will fly by.

||||||||||||||||||||||||||||||||||||||||||||||||||||||||||||||||||||||||||||||||||||||||||||||||||||||||||||||||||||||||||||||||||||||||||||||||||||||||||||||||||

Pre-Play

George was CEO and president of a firm that helps take private companies public. He was his own boss, which, for him, was both a blessing and a curse because he had a hard time staying focused for very long. It would have been easy for him to buy into the attention deficit disorder (ADD) label, but he refused. He knew his problem was a lack of discipline and follow-through, but George didn't know how to stop being that way.

When we met, I realized he was not running his business—it was running him. There was little to no preplanning and no goal setting except keeping the doors open and earning a paycheck.

I helped George get more out of his business by preplanning what needed to be done every day. Under my tutelage, he went from being focused on a paycheck to being focused on daily activity. His income went up almost immediately. Too many people look too far forward to the result, not the activity. But if you don't focus on the right activity, the result is not going to be as good.

Working with an attorney, George helped people go through

the legal morass of setting up a public company. His habit was to show up at work after 9 a.m., sit at his desk for a while, go to lunch, come back, work awhile longer, go to the gym, come back, then slip out and take his kid to Little League. Despite a suspect work ethic, he made decent money. He was getting by. But when he finally realized he was spinning his wheels and wasting his time, he didn't really know what to do.

Working together, we set both short- and long-term goals, and I taught him a technique I call Pre-Play. I use it with athletes and students trying to grasp almost anything. It can help anyone learn faster and better focus on tasks at hand. In George's case, this three-minute daily routine helped increased his revenue 173 percent the first year without adding any extra hours to his day.

The University of California/Irvine had a terrible men's volleyball program until John Speraw took it over in 2003. John read my book and reached out to consult with me. I trained John, then I trained his team. He subsequently led his squads to two NCAA championships. One of the things I taught him was to Pre-Play his practice sessions: Take three minutes out during every practice and visualize what you want to have happen. Now practice. When practice is over, take one minute and replay how practice went. What's one thing you did well? What's one thing you can improve on tomorrow? Then let it go. The result of doing that took the power of the practice and intensified it. Everything was better.

I will ask a softball player, "What do you want to accomplish at practice today?"

She might say, "I want to hit to the opposite field."

Visualize that. What does that look like? How does your swing feel? How do you put the ball there? See and feel where the ball goes for a hit. *Then* go practice.

When practice is over, replay it for a moment. How did you do? Were you putting the ball where you wanted it to go?

As a coach, you'd look ahead to the day and say, "How do I want practice to go today? What's the attitude I want my kids to have? What's the end result? What do I want to have happen at the end of practice?" Pre-Play what that looks like. When it's over, replay it. "How did I do? Did I get closer? Was I further away? What can I do better tomorrow?" Then you're done. Go about your life. When tomorrow comes, Pre-Play practice. Do it all over again.

I did the same thing with George. Pre-Play your day. How do you want it to go? What do you want to have happen? What's the result of your day? When the day is over, take a minute and replay it. Look back: "What did I do right? What's something I have to do better tomorrow?" That little exercise immediately increased George's productivity.

Everybody—owners, supervisors, managers, customer service reps, teachers, secretaries—needs to Pre-Play their day for a successful and productive experience. If you're in sales, what's the first thing you do in your office every morning? Pick up the sports page? Sit at your desk and read it? Go to the water cooler? Get a cup of coffee? That's typical. Do you want to do what successful people do? Is the number one sales person in your office doing that? Probably not.

Some of the activities that were common to you in the past probably are not the way to be successful in the future. This brings us back to patterning on success. What does the successful salesperson in your office—the one who is always leading the weekly sales competition—do when he or she comes in? You're making $40,000 a year, but the guy across the room is making $100,000. Observe how he spends *his* day.

Pre-Play what you need to do. Maybe you need to say, "I'm going to read the sports page and get right on the phone. I'm going to make one hundred phone calls a day. I'm going to see twelve people." Pre-Play those activities the way you would do them if you were an excellent performer on the job. Now go through your day. When the day's over, look back at it. It takes just one minute. "What did I do right? How close was I to my game plan? What's one thing I can do better tomorrow?" Then forget about it, knowing you'll do it again the next day.

If you don't know the right actions, you have to pretend. And the way you pretend is by finding somebody who has the right actions for the task at hand and then patterning their excellence. It might initially be overwhelming to have the habits of the number one guy, so look for one thing you can do differently today.

Don't do the morning water cooler chitchat. Cut that one out and see what happens to your productivity. That alone might add fifteen minutes back to the productivity of your day. (Be prepared to be heckled, however, because your colleagues will notice your absence. They might tease or taunt you about being "too good" for hanging out with them. And one day soon you will be.)

Tomorrow, don't read the whole sports page, scan it and move on. That's probably another fifteen minutes.

Maybe you can eavesdrop a little on the more successful salespeople in the office. Maybe one might let you shadow her on a day's calls. What are some of the things she says to people when cold-calling? How does she handle your sales manager differently than you do? How does she use the Internet and email differently than you do?

A lot of successful people like to have their ego stroked. "Dave, how the heck do you do that? How do you make $100,000 a year?

What's just one of the keys?" Most of the time, Dave is going to tell you, because it makes him feel good. You're not a threat. Dave may not tell you where the gold mine is, but he might tell you how he found it.

The people that have your habits are going to have your income. The people who have smarter practices and make better decisions about applying their time are running laps around you on payday.

People can change. People *do* change. Core personality traits are more difficult. Activities are easier. Daily action plans and to-do lists can help change your activities. It may not be your core persona, but if you know what needs to be done and you remember that successful people do what needs to be done whether they want to or not, you will change your activities.

Make daily adjustments and let them grow into new habits that open a path to increased success. Your productivity will go off the charts. It's a powerful technique.

The Six-Step Power Sequence

Now that we have our champions' attitude, and understand the concept of Pre-Playing a task, let's put it into action. The following six blocks are held together with an "I Can" attitude and give you tremendous power to execute a task. This is an excellent foundation for a sales or public speaking experience.

I created the following sequence to allow everyone to experience both the Mental Edge and the power of Mind Over Business. The sequence is specific, as it uses one sense after another in rapid fashion to cause a positive change in behavior and action.

1. **Say it.** This is about triggering the auditory part of the brain, the verbal part, where you're hearing what you're saying while you are saying it. Say what you are going to do. "I am going to convince and motivate." "I will close and make the sale."

2. **See it.** Saying it primes the brain for imagery. See yourself give a convincing, motivating speech that propels your audience to act on what you say. See positive head nods and smiling faces all during the presentation. See yourself making the sale. See the client enjoying the experience. See your skillful close as you ask for the order and hand the client a pen and receive, in return, a signed contract and check.

3. **Feel it.** Notice your confident posture as you give the speech. Feel your facial expressions; be aware of your hands gesturing. Experience the post-speech moments with people congratulating you and responding positively. Feel the commitment to the close as you hand the client a pen. Feel the pen go from your hand to theirs and it is so strong you actually feel it and the sound it makes as it goes across the paper. Finish with a firm, confident handshake.

4. **Do it.** With full commitment, take action. Legendary Los Angeles Dodgers manager Tommy Lasorda said he would rather a pitcher commit 100 percent to the wrong pitch than 97 percent to the right pitch. Why? Because a 100 percent commitment is *that* powerful. You know more than your audience or clients because you arrived prepared, mentally and physically. Take on the posture of a winner and let yourself go. No worries, no fear, just do.

5. **Reinforce it.** After the action has been completed and you succeeded, reinforce it. Reinforce positive results with a performance cue to anchor these feelings. It can be as simple as

saying a cue word like "Yes!" and making a fist as you say it. During a volleyball match, my daughter would go back to serve. I would yell out to her, "See it!" which began her on the track of say it, see it, feel it, do it. She would instantly tell herself where she was putting the ball. She would see the ball land there and feel her contact and the arm swing that would make the ball go there, and then she'd do it. When the serve was over and she got what she wanted, without anybody knowing what she was doing, she would make a fist and say to herself, "Yes, that's me!" and every time she would have a success she would use that cue, stacking success upon success, conditioning the cue so she could Pre-Play it to get into a peak performance state before important matches or points. When the speech or sales call goes well, stack the cue! Use a word or short phrase and repeat it with intensity while applying a physical cue.

6. **Dismiss it.** When you don't get what you want, learn from it and let it go. When my daughter didn't get the serve she wanted, she would dismiss it with a simple "That's not me. I am better than that!" and then brush it away with her off hand as if to say, "I don't own that result." But she would always learn from it. Maybe she dropped her elbow? She would say, "Next time elbow high and feel the high elbow." When speeches and sales don't go well, brush it off. "That's not me. I am better than that! Next time I will be better organized. Next time I will have better rapport and the close will be easier."

I see people stacking negative anchors all the time. When something goes wrong, they hit their forehead. Or they're driving down the road, and somebody cuts them off. There's the backward wave with one finger. "You SOB!!!" and they stack it. They are *looking* for things to go wrong. Yet when something goes right, when they are driving down the freeway and somebody lets them in, they don't say, "Hallelujah! Praise the Lord, that lovely woman let me in!" That, they take for granted.

We stack negative all the time, we take the positive for granted.

The person who got cut off always shows up at the office upset, starting the day in a bad mood: "Somebody cut me off, they almost *killed* me!" This person holds on to that negative experience for ten, fifteen, twenty minutes, maybe the whole morning. Yet, the same day, maybe twice on the way to work, somebody let the same person into busy traffic. But the response to that was not "Life is great. I love people! That guy let me in!" People don't come walking into the office jumping up on their toes and waving their hands in celebration of the selfless act someone unleashed on them. Yet they do in response to something negative.

The idea behind creating new reality is stacking the positive and minimizing and eliminating the negative. They are both just as real. It's your choice. Again, we're back to life being a mind game in which *you* make the rules.

Reinforcing your attitude with positive results gives you more power. How the power sequence blocks are laid out determines the outcome. There are six blocks here; if any of them are missing, you're not going to benefit from the full power of the *six*-step power sequence. It will be like a six-cylinder engine running on four or five cylinders; it will still go, but the ride won't be as smooth or efficient.

Give Your Undivided Attention to the Right Thing

There are so many distractions every day! There is paperwork to do, meetings to attend, an avalanche of memos to send and reports to be written. But what's the most important thing in your day? What really drives your business?

I'll never forget Elvin. He was an insurance agent in Omaha, Nebraska. Incredibly organized. This guy's files had files. Everything was in perfect order.

"Elvin, how ya doing today?"

"Just getting organized."

"How ya doing, Elvin?"

"Oh, just getting organized."

He sat right next to me. Elvin was the most organized guy in the office, but he almost never sold a thing. The guy was the worst salesman in the office! How he stayed—or even *why* he stayed—in that office year after year, I don't know. He was making about $170 a week and already in his late forties.

His attention was focused on the wrong thing. He didn't understand that being organized wasn't making him any money!

How do we give our undivided attention to the important things? What's job number one? What's job number two? What's job number three? Make a daily to-do list of the priority requirements of your daily routine. Number one should always be the one that leads to the bottom line. Number two should be the second one in line to the bottom line.

Too many times, the to-do list has to do with things that are important to *you*, not to the bottom line.

If you don't have a goal, what are you doing every day?

So you have a goal and a to-do list—now you've got something to focus on.

Rodrigo Gonzales was a three-time all-American swimmer at UCLA facing his last competitive swim meet. More than anything, he wanted to break into the top sixteen finalists at the Pan American Games in Cuba that year. He had never, ever cracked the top sixteen in his life. That group is elite, and after qualifying rounds, it includes the only athletes who swim on the last day of competition. If you're not in the sixteen, you're not a swimmer, you're a spectator.

It was the last swim meet of his life, and Rodrigo hired me to help him get the Mental Edge. With practice, he used Pre-Play to race, in his mind, within a tenth to a hundredth of a second of his speed in the upcoming race, that's how focused he was. When we started, his goal was to be in the top sixteen. By our third session, he wanted to be in the top three. He thought he could earn at least a bronze medal.

I said, "Are you sure you can do it?"

"Yes!" he said.

He went to Cuba for the Pan American Games, swam his race at exactly the time he did in Pre-Play and won the bronze medal by one-hundredth of a second. It was fingernail close—the guy who had the longest fingernails won.

That's the value of your undivided attention. Rodrigo didn't get distracted by "What if this happens? What if that happens? What if others swim faster? What if I don't feel good?" None of that got in his dome.

He focused on what he *could* do, not on his limitations, not on worries and not on the competition, and that was the biggie. Rodrigo did not get distracted by "What if this happens, what if that happens, what if others . . ." He gave his attention to his start, to his stroke, to his finish, to his time—that's where he spent his mental energy. He practiced accordingly, and he got it right.

When I am rock climbing, everything else shuts down. There is nothing but me and that rock face and the next hold. The only success is going up. There is no success in going down: that's failure. And you can fail really, really hard.

Never worry about falling—worry about the sudden stop!

When I am rock climbing, I look at every possible irregularity in the rock as a grab, as a hold. I remember examining pictures of my friend Mark climbing. He was sprawled out on a rock, limbs all akimbo.

"Mark," I asked, "how do you get to the next hold?"

"Right there," he said, pointing to a spot only he could see, "there's this juicy hold about the size of a nickel. I have no choice but to succeed. Falling is not an option."

When I climb, nothing else matters. On the side of a giant rock, I'm not a writer, I'm not a trainer, I'm not a father, I'm nothing but a guy on a rock looking for any irregularity in the rock to keep me safe. That's undivided attention at its best.

I have seen people texting on rocks while their buddy is up on the other end of the rope. If it were my climbing partner, I'd slap that guy silly.

I fell hard once, climbing a crack in California's Joshua Tree National Park. It happened so fast. To this day, it blows me away how fast it happened, and I thought I was in a good spot. Fortunately, it was early in the climb, and I landed on my crash pad. I hit the side of the rock, got bruised up pretty good, but I was fortunate. It was the result of a split-second lack of concentration caused by thinking ahead and also my attention being diverted as someone was taking my picture. A little thing like that can cause a disaster. I was locked in and focused, and then one minor distraction changed my focus in an instant and down I went.

Be Calm Under Any Pressure

When you get tense, your posture changes. Your shoulders have a tendency to rise, your breathing gets high in the chest, and as a result, you are not thinking as clearly.

Some pressure is good. NBA legend and Naismith Memorial Basketball Hall of Famer Magic Johnson would take the pressure of the NBA finals, and it would grace his game, because he didn't feel it in a negative way.

How you view a situation determines whether it's pressure or not. A basketball game is a basketball game is a basketball game. It never changes. It's the same game whether it's game one of the NBA season or Game One of the NBA Finals. The court's the same, the ball's the same, five guys on a team, same referees, the ESPN cameras are always present to record your brilliance as well as your misfires.

What's the difference?

It's the expectancy of the prize. If that makes you play better, by all means, feel that way. If it doesn't make you play better, just let it be another game. Pressure only comes from within.

To relax under pressure, you need to realize what makes you tick, what makes you flow. "Oh my gosh, I've got to get one more sale or I'm going to get fired!" Is that going to motivate you, or is it "If I get one more sale, I will be salesperson of the week"?

There is a popular story—probably an urban legend—that illustrates this point, true or not. A dejected salesman leaves home to take one more crack at his territory. He knows full well that he is on the verge of getting fired because he's not performing. As he flies off, his wife kisses him and hugs him and says, "Honey, I believe in you."

He lands at his destination, picks up a rental car and reluctantly gets to work. As usual, it's not going well.

His wife calls him halfway through the route and says, "How you doing, baby?"

"Not well," he says, dejected. "It's such a struggle."

"Well, you know what? Everything's going to be okay," she says. "We won the lottery! Sixteen million bucks!"

He's excited, she's excited, he's stoked.

"That's incredible! I have to finish my route, but I'll be home on Friday and we'll celebrate!"

Friday was two days away, so—being the responsible yet unproductive salesperson he was—he finished his route without a care in the world, the best two days of his life. No worries, no fear—he didn't *have* to make a sale, so he just went out and had a good time with people. And the people who encountered him for the next two days actually bought what he was selling for the first time!

His boss loved him again. "I don't know how you turned it around," the boss said, "but you get to keep your job now."

"I don't want the job, I quit!"

He flew home, gave his wife a bear hug and said, "Baby, let me see the lottery ticket."

"Aw, honey, you were feeling so bad, you were so down in the dumps, I just said that to make you feel better. There is no lottery ticket."

What makes a person respond well? *Perception*. The situation didn't change. But the salesman's perception of the situation altered drastically because of that good news. The idea is we don't want to worry, we want to *do*. Don't worry in advance. Fortune-telling causes, for most people, negative emotion and paralysis. Some people are motivated by negative imagery and negative consequences, but it's a painful way to live. *Life is a mind game, and you make the rules.*

Plan, Plan, Plan

Throughout this book, I've talked you through the hurdles I have jumped to get where I am today. We're all flawed, and I've exposed more than a few of my own imperfections. Here's one more: I'm not a good guy at making daily activity lists. Lots of people I know are wonderful about doing them, and I need to be one of those people because when I write action lists I always get more done. The key is, first things first.

It's a constant struggle for me. I'm a big-picture guy. That's the way my brain operates. I realize now that such a list is pretty important because, like you, I'm always so busy. When I was younger, I never thought twice about preparing a to-do list. I didn't like to do paperwork. I was focused on just the bottom line. Can't do that anymore! I have to have a schedule; I have to know what I'm doing, and when I'm going to do it. This is a perfect task for the computer, the PDA, the smartphone, the iPhone or the iPad. I'd be dead in the water without electronic scheduling.

Part of the challenge is that as we get older, the memory gets a little soft. Once upon a time, it was easy to remember a couple appointments a day. Today, forget about it!

You have to be organized in our flash-forward world, and learning that has helped me tremendously. It used to be that when things were filed, I couldn't find them, because I was used to my office life being disorganized. Now I treasure a logical filing system and knowing where things are at all times.

Successful people do what needs to be done, whether they want to or not. I had to force myself into being more organized and to be a better planner of "Ken Baum, Inc." To accomplish that, the imagination is more important than willpower, so I imagined myself being more organized; I saw myself knowing where things were kept. I started giving audio cues to the things I was doing, as simple as "I'm putting my keys on the hook," "I'm putting my wallet here," "I'm putting the file over there."

I visualized myself being an organized, collected person who no longer let my creativity become an excuse for being unorganized. I'm not perfect, but I am much more efficient.

Your commitment to focus and concentration will allow you to get more done in less time and improve the quality of your work.

8

Making a New Reality

MAXIMUM PERFORMANCE STATE

At this point, I hope you have embraced the *Mind Over Business* concept and gone through all the rational thought processes that help the mind control the body—and help you take charge of your own mind. You've learned the exercises. You see that perception matters, that attitude matters. Now, how do you take all that and get into peak performance?

Maximum Performance State (MPS) is not a motivational practice; it's an internal skill. At this point, I will teach you how to take all your visualizations, all your breathing exercises, all your self-talk, posture and feelings, and put them together in an anchor you can use to get in a peak performance state, so that you can get the job done and get it done every time. This chapter is about getting yourself in that state whether you want to or not, whether you feel good or feel bad, whether things are going well or going poorly.

I've heard it said, "Don't let the bastards get you down." This is the time when you learn a skill so that, externally, nobody can tell if the bastards are getting to you or not, and, more importantly, internally you are not faking it, you actually believe this way. You have developed an undying *Mind Over Business* belief that you will succeed.

One of the main reasons people don't change is because they're afraid. There is an innate fear for many of us in doing something different.

FEAR!

Albert was one of twenty-eight people in a class I taught on public speaking. And out of those twenty-eight people, every one had a discomfort to a greater or lesser degree about making presentations. All the FEAR—False Evidence As Real—was in their heads. It was their reality that was the problem. It wasn't the other person's reality; it was their own.

To get over this, we talked about the structure of presentations. I asked students not to stand but to comment from their seat about something, anything about which they were confident, such as "What do you do for a living?" "I'm a CPA." They were sitting; nobody was looking askance at them. In that way we broke down the experience.

We graduated from sitting to standing, still at the seat, followed by a more complicated question. "You're a CPA? How many years have you been doing it?"

"Thirty-two years."

Then they separated into little groups and began small group conversations. They soon were standing at the front of the class without a prepared speech, just talking, making conversation with the group about things they knew and didn't need notes to discuss.

Before they ever gave a real speech, they went through the relaxation techniques and how to breathe, putting themselves in a positive state, followed by my Six-Step Power Sequence from Chapter 7: *say it, see it, feel it, do it, reinforce it* or *dismiss it*. In an instant, it allows people to do the things they need to do to change their internal and external state to a more positive one, as their posture, imagery, self-talk and breathing all change. Results are immediately different.

Albert came to me with a problem: although he was one of the most intelligent people I ever met, he was deathly afraid of public speaking. He was living in fear. It made him feel like a failure, even though he was a successful accountant, well respected in his Iowa hometown, a true business leader. He always had the content; he never had the confidence. All the usual tricks and mind games left him even more frustrated because they didn't work for him.

Albert was a small-town boy who didn't feel as intelligent as he was and who worried so much about making mistakes or saying the wrong thing that he would just freeze when he got up in front of a group of anything more than three people—friends or strangers, it didn't matter. It wouldn't even have to be a speech, it could just be a round-robin discussion. He couldn't speak up.

"Whoever came up with the idea of 'imagine your audience naked' should be shot!" he said.

I agreed. "You don't need a trick; you need to change your mind and create a new reality, Albert."

I told him to start by using his past success and combine it with a future pace so he could thoroughly enjoy public speaking and give his audience the value of his experience and education.

I guaranteed him we would use no tricks to achieve a major breakthrough—and we did not. It started with a history search that allowed us to tap into how he thought and how he had achieved success in the past. He would then take these feelings, postures and images and tie them to a word—his word was "worthy"—and a physical cue—grabbing his left thumb's knuckle—that he could replay for every speech.

Albert's son wrote me a heartfelt letter that said, in part, "I want to tell you, you made my dad feel so good. Public speaking has been a lifelong fear of his, and you helped him get over it. I can't thank you enough."

Albert created a new reality, because his old reality wasn't working. He didn't just put on a happy face, he didn't just tough it out, he changed the way he thought, which changed the way he acted.

Expect Your Best

Your mind is the only limit that your body knows. It's the most important thing in getting beyond where you are right now. With mental training, you can become the person you choose to be.

Before you step foot into your office again—or wherever you work—picture yourself having the impact on people you've only dreamt about. See yourself getting the job done and finally earning the support of your coworkers. You have a much better chance of this happening if you visualize yourself as successful than if you continue to see yourself as an average person having to beg for your coworkers' cooperation. Make your internal images strong and personal and then present yourself the way you want to be. Set your sights high.

The more you expect from yourself, the more you will achieve. In sports, the team that is behind in the game but expects to rally and come back always plays better than a team that is just trying to not be embarrassed.

A worker who is doing everything he or she can to be employee of the month will outwork and outperform the person who is just trying to get by. Modest expectations produce modest results.

But when you focus on the possibility of real success, your enthusiasm peaks, your senses become sharper, and memories of success remind you of actions that work. This act alone—high expectancy—will move you a giant step closer to reaching your potential. Then, by maintaining high expectancy, you'll overcome setbacks more quickly and decisively as you pursue your goal.

When you communicate directly with yourself this way, you'll be better able to shatter the limits that others have put on you or those that are self-imposed. Use the success history search before learning anything new, or when you are assigned a task about which you're less than confident. Each time you do, your unconscious mind will build on its past successes, activating all your resources and improving your chance of future success.

This technique literally reestablishes old connections between body and brain, strengthening memories between the mind and muscles that can be replayed every time you need to get a job done. In the days ahead, when you're challenged, not feeling good, perhaps running on empty with no sleep, you can call upon these positive images to get you into your personal MPS.

Brains learn best from images. The more intense and the more positive they are, the better. It's imperative to fill your mind with positive—not negative—images. There is a time when negative imagery is powerful, but not now. I teach athletes that they need to have a Kobe Bryant attitude—don't think about your misses, think about your makes—and the next shot will drop in. *Swoosh!* You don't want to give your mind and body any messages contrary to what you want to have happen. If you do, you'll set up an internal battle that will get in the way of success.

Negative examples might include:

- "I don't want to blow this chance."
- "I don't want to strike out."

Positive examples could be:

- "I will capitalize on this chance."
- "I will get a hit."

The success history search gives your mind a track to run on, and your body will follow. It's like the conductor of an orchestra. All the musicians know the music, but unless the conductor harmonizes it, it will never come out right. The conductor and the musicians practice together by repeatedly going over the songs so they are hitting the right notes at the right time. When the curtain rises on opening night, beautiful music erupts to the delight of the crowd, and the orchestra finishes every movement to a thundering ovation.

Your big moment is every morning when you wake up and you have a choice: Are you going to conduct a beautiful symphony or just show up and hope to slide through another day?

THE CIRCLE OF EXCELLENCE

The Circle of Excellence is a great exercise that creates a cocoon of focus and concentration and precipitates positive, proactive steps. It was another part of the puzzle I used with Albert.

This exercise ties together physical and verbal performance cues, posture and past success to anchor you to feelings and thoughts of success, allowing you to "lock in" focused activity and "lock out" distractions. This advanced use of imagery will put you in a peak state ready for exceptional performance. You first need to download the information, tied to a specific cue. This can then be replayed in an instant. You will do a series of things before you have to recall it: relive past experiences; heighten successes to the next level. But it takes time. That's the installation; that's what stepping into the circle represents. Once it's installed, you walk to the lectern, imagine it, say your word and your cue, and you're on your way.

Find a comfortable place in which you can stand without distractions. The exercise will consist of reliving three past successful experiences using all possible senses. You will imagine a colored circle in front of you that you will step into. The circle can be any color and can be flat on the ground; there could be a small step up or a step such as you would find up to an Olympic Gold Medal stand. Your circle can have sides that go up like the "Beam me up, Scotty!" transporter from *Star Trek*. There is no preferred circle, so let your mind create the one that's right for you. Later your circle might evolve to form a rectangle like I use with baseball players so they step into the batter's box, or a colored lectern like I use with public speaking. For now, let's work with a circle.

To start, stand in a comfortable position. Take a deep, gentle breath. Exhale and breathe normally. After a few more breaths, proceed the following way:

In your mind, go back to a time when you were younger, whether a few days ago, a month ago or a year ago. Focus on an experience that you had that made you feel really good about yourself and your ability to succeed. (It could be an experience you used in earlier exercises.) It may have occurred in business, school, sports or any time in the course of your life. Notice what pops into your head. How did it make you feel when you knew you were successful? What do you see? What do you hear? What do you smell or taste? As you relive this event notice how your imagery is much clearer than before. You're able to relive experiences like this more vividly than you did when you first used visualization.

Now go to another time, when you were younger still and you got the results you wanted and felt really good about it. Re-experience it as though it were happening now. Become aware of the expression on your face. What were you thinking? What was the tone of voice you used inside your head? How did you stand; what was your posture? Notice any smells or tastes associated with this success. How good does this memory make you feel? Feel your posture *now*.

Think of a third experience, farther back in your past, an experience that made you feel good about being you. Maybe it was overcoming a challenge, something you were apprehensive or scared of but you did anyway and excelled. Remember the feelings of confidence and joy! See yourself doing that *now*. What do you see? What are the dominant colors? Notice the sounds around you. Become aware of any familiar tastes or smells. Feel your winning posture as you say, "Yes, this is *me*!"

Next let's build a performance cue. What is a word that describes these three, stacked successes? It can be any word, such as "Fantastic!" or "Powerful!" Use one word when possible. It could even be as simple as "Yes!" or as profound as a football player I know who says, "I am the *shit*!" This cue, when experienced through emotion and belief, will trigger positive emotions and corresponding posture that will lead to future success.

Picture an imaginary circle in front of you. It is *your* circle of excellence. Take a moment to look at it closely. What color is your circle? Is it flat on the ground, or elevated? Are there sides to it? Does it go from ceiling to floor? What is unique about your circle? Envision a clear, vivid image of your personal circle. It is unique to you. Before you step into it, quickly line up your three success images. Then step into it. It will intensify all past feelings of success and remind your mind and body that you *can* succeed.

When you step into your circle, your past successes become even more powerful. Your circle will become a cocoon of concentration and will instantly fire up all the memories in your brain, and that will cause you to perform better.

Inside the circle, the volume of your self-talk and external world are at the perfect level for sending powerful signals to your brain. The images have just the right brightness and color to stimulate right actions. *Now* is the time to physically step forward into your personal circle of excellence. In your imagination, step into your personal circle of excellence. As you do, say your cue word out loud, with passion and true belief. At that same moment, allow all the feelings about those past successes to intensify. Everything you experience will become more acute, giving you a sharp feeling of "Yes, I can!" As your images and feelings reach a fevered peak, feel as if you put them in your dominant hand, then squeeze your fist and pump it forcefully as you say your cue word. Do this three times and, after each time, pause a few seconds to allow your emotions to soar. Stand with the posture of excellence as you soak in all of your life's learning. Finally, step out of the circle of excellence.

It's not uncommon to feel like a million bucks, that you can lick the world, after this exercise. It's also not uncommon to be overwhelmed with emotion and shed a tear or two as you break through current limitations of negativity, realizing "Yes, I can!"

I have used this exercise with equal effectiveness with businesspeople and athletes. Two athletes stand out because, although their responses to the circle were completely different, it caused each to perform better. One football player who had been cut the year before and was suffering from self-doubt and negativity, stepped into his circle and cried like a baby. This big, strong, tough guy was overcome with emotion as he realized he wasn't the bad player some coaches had made him out to be. His being cut didn't take away from his potential. This was his breakthrough, and he went on to the next season's training camp and made an NFL roster.

The second athlete played at the highest Olympic level. *He* thought the exercise was silly and childish. But after the experience of literally stepping into it, he went on to use his circle-of-excellence experience in the heat of competition to register the best performances of his life.

You, too, can use the circle of excellence to break through limitations, negativity, nervousness or anxieties so you can perform when the pressure is on and have the kind of genuine confidence and real self-esteem that says, "Yes, I can!"

Maximum Performance State

The MPS I seek for athletes can also be a business state of mind. This is a way to be, a way to think. This is a way to act. Most people never get there, because they don't know how, and most people who teach motivation don't know how to teach it, because it's not a motivational thing, it's an internal thing.

All people who are called on to perform, whether in business or sports, will get a better result when they get into their MPS. It's the moment when everything clicks. It's that state of mind when everything is working, what some people call "the zone." It's when the mind and body are working in perfect harmony, focused and locked in with an almost semiconscious euphoria that facilitates peak performance. When they give a speech, the words flow, motivating, educating and entertaining their audience. When they write a report, the knowledge flows out of them as if from another source. Everything comes effortlessly.

Now that you've done all of the exercises in this book, you have the power to move yourself to MPS on a consistent basis. By doing the cue, saying the word, changing the posture, you'll be able to reach MPS in an instant. It can be accomplished easily, and it won't require a huge time commitment. Choose the exercises that work best for you and apply them immediately and daily. You've begun to integrate *Mind Over Business* techniques into your daily activity. In the process, you've made great gains in creating harmony between your mind and body.

The Power of Consistent, Resilient Action

Motivation can be fleeting. You see it in gyms all over America and in diets that start with gusto and end with a binge—in my experience, initial motivation lasts an average of about seventeen days. In training people from every walk of life, I find that the difference between success or failure is that successful people know how to stay motivated for more than seventeen days.

Since enthusiasm and motivation tend to naturally wane over time, you need to do something to keep your eye on the prize. To keep motivation high, you need to keep refueling the tank. Think of personal drive in the same way you would the engine of a car and make motivation its accelerator. I always stress to my clients the importance of Consistent Resilient Action (CRA). It is really more than just action; it is action pursued by a made-up mind, causing an internal drive that creates excitement and commitment and never lets up. Through Mindsetting you can develop enthusiasm and passion for a business plan or a new goal that you can stick with . . . no matter what. CRA keeps your Desire Statement front and center. Read it daily and stick to the path that you've chosen!

Let's heighten your passion and create more resolve by connecting to your dream and turning it into reality. Rewrite your Desire Statement with "I will" rather than "I want to." This may trigger subtle or obvious changes in your feelings and emotions.

MY DESIRE STATEMENT

I will:

_____

_____

You need desire in order to develop the drive to reach your goals, but not everyone has a strong enough desire to fuel a powerful internal drive. These men and women have more of a *wish* than a true desire.

When the desire is real, however, it is the focus of all your attention and energy. It will become your dominant thought and can push you toward achieving your goal. Just how far can desire take you? How about from janitor to speaker of the House? In January 2011, John Boehner became the third most powerful person in America even though he came from the humblest of beginnings. One of eleven children in a one-bathroom house, he paid his way through college by toiling as a night janitor. It took him seven years to put himself through school, but he never stopped reaching for accomplishments that everyone else said were beyond his grasp.

Desire is the great equalizer. We all know smart kids that never fulfilled their potential. Or athletes with tremendous talent who never performed up to their ability.

What about *you*? CRA can compensate for many shortcomings in your talent. If you're willing to work harder than was your previous custom and stick to your personal and mental training program, you can enjoy more success than you've ever dreamed possible. When others are wasting time with long, drawn-out water-cooler conversations, you'll be creating positive self-talk. While others are vegging out in front of the television from the time they get home until bedtime, you'll be creating positive images in your mind. Even if you weren't blessed with the best situation, looks, voice or background, you can bless yourself with CRA and grow a desire and drive that is second to none.

Success is much easier once you believe that you can achieve it, and, in fact, all of your business and personal goals will be within reach. CRA allows you to have the MPS on a consistent basis. We all know people who fly high then come crashing down. CRA is about living your MPS on a regular basis. All of us get the wind kicked out of us, but we have to come back. CRA keeps us in that state.

9

Break Out of Your Comfort Zone

I often ask men and women before I train them, "What's more important to you, comfort or effectiveness?" They might say effectiveness, but they almost always go for comfort. People don't like to go out of their comfort zone. I teach them the value of getting out of that comfort zone and give them techniques to force them out of it:

- "You don't like making phone calls? Well, let's make a hundred today—with a smile on your face."
- "You don't like meeting people? Meet three a day for the next two weeks."
- "You don't like doing squats? Today we'll start on an intense squat program."

Change comes from stretching yourself. Be what you haven't

been before. I exaggerate the change. Little, bitty, minor adjustments in ourselves that take too long won't do because it's easy to slip back into the same ineffective habits. We want to get you out of your comfort zone. The whole idea of *Mind Over Business* is to become what you haven't been before, and to do that, you have to break out of your comfort zone. Train to be great. Success or comfort, I ask—which do *you* want?

Success or Comfort?

I sometimes find myself working with an athlete whose body is out of balance. Typically, it's because he focused on what he liked to do, the repetitions and exercises that are comfortable for him. For instance, it's typical for athletes to excel at what they're good at doing. Their arms grow well, so they do lots of curls and look good in a tank top. However, their calves are stubborn, so they hide them with sweatpants or long socks and don't work on them. Before his competitive bodybuilding phase, Arnold Schwarzenegger had weak, skinny calves that were holding him back. Instead of hiding his calves, he cut off all of his sweatpants at the knee to fully expose his weakness and turn it into a motivation. He opted for success and became Mr. Olympia. Oh, and a movie star. And married into the Kennedy dynasty. And became governor of California.

If you prefer comfort to success, chances are you are in the wrong business or should expect to hit a plateau. You need to blast out of your comfort zone until you feel comfortable again. In sports and fitness training, the body gets sore as lactic acid builds up and muscle fiber is stressed. If what you're doing feels comfortable, then you didn't go through your comfort zone. If what you're doing is easy, you're still in your comfort zone. Eventually, if you really push the envelope, you're not going to feel comfortable doing what you're doing. At some point, it will become more comfortable, you will become more skilled, and your body and mind will adapt to being that way. To continue the growth, you must go through this process again.

Some people are comfortable being salespeople or being a leader or a manager and giving a presentation. People who aren't effective or successful represent the kind of comfort I'm combatting. If you are the CEO of a $100 million company and you are comfortable doing what you do, well, then, by all means keep doing what you do if it works for you and the people who rely upon you. But when you're not successful—when your shareholders aren't happy—that's when you should ask yourself, "Am I too comfortable?"

There are so many people who refuse to change the way they are. "I can't change me, it's just the way I am." Well, everybody can change. When it gets right down to it, a lot of people think the way they are is the right way to be. That's why they're that way. If it weren't the right way to be, they would change. When they wake up in the morning, they are not thinking, "You know what? I'm going to screw up my life today. I am going to be ineffective." When they wake up in the morning, they think they are living the life that's right for them. This is the way they are. "I like myself this way, because I'm comfortable. That's why I wake up and smoke cigarettes and drink a bunch of coffee. Even though I know it's not the right thing to do, I'm comfortable that way. I'm drinking a beer on the couch right now and it's only 8 a.m. But I'm *comfortable*."

Typically, whatever you are comfortable with is putting you where you are right now. As I said earlier, if you keep doing the same things, you'll get the same results—whether you like them or not.

What makes you comfortable doesn't necessarily make you effective. It's like sitting on your favorite couch. It may be comfortable, it may be molded to your butt shape after time, but it may not be the best ergonomic choice for your anatomy. If you sit with good posture, you could be really uncomfortable. Your body will rebel and might even feel weird as the muscles and skeleton are positioned properly. Eventually, if you go for effectiveness, you've got to break that posture and change it. Eventually, that change will feel comfortable.

To be effective, you have to make either incremental movement with CRA toward effectiveness or—preferably—big jumps, quantum leaps. People are different in what they can handle. In the last chapter I talked about Albert's public speaking challenges. When he started by sitting in his chair saying what he did for a living, then stood up, then joined a small group, and ultimately stood up before the class, that was the real thing. Step by step, Albert broke out of *his* comfort zone.

Think of this: When you opt for fitness as opposed to being a couch potato, you start working muscle. To make any muscle grow, you have to make it uncomfortable. You've got to make it burn. As a result, the muscle adapts and changes. Once it adapts and changes, you get status quo. It gets used to using a thirty-pound barbell for a curl, which initially made it sore. But that soreness represented the muscle growing. Then it stopped. As soon as the muscle got comfortable, it stopped growing. The answer? You add five pounds more, or two more reps. The muscle will get fatigued again, uncomfortable, and it burns. It is growing again. The body is made to consistently challenge itself to go beyond where it is and where it has been. That's where growth comes from. Growth is often uncomfortable—remember the way your body ached as a teen when you were going through growth spurts?

The same thing is true of mental growth. You must consistently challenge the brain to go beyond self-imposed limits. If you are doing everything easily, and it's all smooth sailing, you are not challenging yourself. That means you are probably missing out on something that will make you more effective.

Knowledge is cumulative; one thing leads to another. Where does insight come from? What about creativity? Usually, they both stem from a knowledge base. If you don't have the knowledge base, what can you create? There is no paint on your palette. You need the knowledge base, which becomes stacked and cumulative.

Let's address a specific sales skill such as cold-calling potential clients.

Practice by making a phone call to a stranger. Don't worry about saying the right thing; just change the name of the company. They don't know who you are; they will hang up and forget about you. But when *you* hang up, you will remember every grueling second of that dial, possibly for the rest of your life. Forget about it; laugh about it. It doesn't matter. Now make a hundred real calls. Get on a roll, and don't judge anything. Just see what happens. That's the way I teach salespeople to use the phone.

Sometimes, you need to focus on negative movements—the eccentric or downward motion of a bench press—to create greater muscle growth. In many cases we can grow more from negative events that occur than positive ones.

Eccentric movement recruits more muscle fiber for more growth, and also more soreness. After doing it, you need more time to recover. Sometimes when people are put in a negative situation, they grow from it if they understand that this is part of a process. If they don't understand that, it's painful, it's brutal, so therein lies the reason for the free calls to strangers that grant a salesperson a license to mess up.

I Dare You: Change!

I mentioned earlier that most people stop changing by the time they're out of high school or college. They lock in young with "This is the way I am," as if it's wrong to change. We've all heard somebody say, "I've been doing this for my whole life." Does that make it valid? No, it doesn't. You can be smoking your whole life. Does that make it good for you? People wear their lack of change like a badge of honor, whether it's hair or religion. They don't question why they are the way they are, even if it limits them.

Almost every salesperson that's ever failed is in that category. Salespeople come to a business all excited about selling the widget of the day. They want to sell the widget the way they think they can do it, because it's comfortable for them. When they learn that's not the way successful people do it, they're gone. Entrepreneurs might build a really great IT consulting business and then decide to start a restaurant, just the way they did the consulting business. Why? "Because I like me this way. I was successful, so why change?" But running a restaurant is a completely different business, requiring different strategies, different skills, and completely different go-to databases.

People that fail do so because they are not willing to venture out of their comfort zone. They are happy being the way they are. When they lose everything, they have a tendency to cast blame on things beyond their control. "It was the economy." "It was illegal immigrants." "It was this; it was that." In reality, it was *them*.

If you're one of these people, you need to start on a comprehensive comfort zone breakout program. You can do it by putting yourself in positions and circumstances that make you uncomfortable. Learn a musical instrument you've never played before. Play a sport you've never attempted before. Try a gym regimen that's totally new to you.

A skilled martial artist and violinist I know has written on his dojo "shoshin," which conveys the thought of "beginner's mind." In a beginner's mind, there are infinite possibilities; in the expert mind, few. He is one of the most egocentric people I've ever met. He will not do anything but karate and violin, because, he told me, "I don't like to look bad in front of other people."

Talk about the height of hypocrisy—but it is the truth, for him. That's why most people don't get out of their comfort zone. He is a seventh-degree black belt, incredibly talented, but he cannot sustain a functional studio because he won't break out of his comfort zone, he won't go beyond. He's seventy-two years old. His answer to everything is "This is the way I did it back in 1972, and this is still the way I do it now." He loses more students every month because of this behavior.

The beginner's mind is important, and I live that philosophy by always doing new things. I challenge myself constantly, in sports, in business, and life. It's a fun way to live. You have to be careful you don't become a jack-of-all-trades, master of none. When you have a beginner's mind, you may be someone who likes to try everything and, as a result, is not getting good at *any*thing. When it comes to your business, whether you are an accountant or an engineer, a ship's captain or a financial services broker, you need a beginner's mind so that you're open to new ways of doing your job.

And while beginning is great, you must learn to finish. There is incredible power attendant with learning to finish what you start. When I teach people how to run, I always instruct them, "Go through the finish line. Don't just finish, run through it," meaning your finish line is three steps beyond the tape. That model helps people to break out of their comfort zone and learn to take the extra step.

Train to Be Great

It's easier to train for something when you have your eye on being the best you can be and you have your eye on something great.

At the same time, a lot of people, while they appear poised for greatness, are not ready for it. How many times do we hear about people winning the lottery and ruining their lives? They are not ready to be great. They are not ready to have money. They are not ready to have success.

If I had had big success when I was young, I probably would have blown it. I would have screwed everything up, because it would have gone to my head; I would have used the money unwisely, made really bad choices. I wasn't ready to be great.

People need to get themselves in a situation so that when good things happen, they handle them well. Put yourself and success in the future mentally and think about how you will handle it. What will you do with that good fortune of yours? How will you react when good things happen to you?

Make a commitment to filling in your gaps by building the blocks you need for your pyramid of success. Everything you do is either a block or the mortar that holds the blocks together. You need them both.

If you are shy and passive, get a book on assertiveness; read another on confidence. Make it a commitment to read two books on a subject. With at least two, you will get more than one viewpoint on how to handle something. Listen to audio programs; download things to your iPod every day. Go online to MindOverBusiness.com each week for my "Mental Edge Minute." There will always be something to get you into a new state.

Training to be great means taking your schedule and saying, "How can I add five minutes of quality work to my day? How can I add twenty minutes or an hour? How can I close my day more effectively?" That's training to be great. It's getting feedback or finding a qualified mentor and asking in earnest, "What can I do better?" Ask a colleague, "How can we do this as a team?"

I see it work in fitness all the time. The buddy system keeps people on task. I have clients who never before got up at seven in the morning to be at the gym by eight for the sole purpose of superhard training. Alone, they would never hear of it, but once they have a partner, they've made a commitment to a friend. We actually partner people up, and we don't always partner people up by similarity. We partner them up based on who we think will work well with somebody else. They are required to text or email each other what's going on with their diet and nutrition. They are required to touch base to make sure the other person is going to be at the gym the next morning for the workout. The bodies that we've seen change because of that are phenomenal. Men, women, it doesn't matter.

A forty-something mom of two was a regular in our gym. She made respectable gains, but then she hit a wall; her body was no longer changing. We partnered her up with a woman who was ten years older and a yoga enthusiast. She worked hard, too, but wasn't getting the physical results she had envisioned. We partnered these two women in an intense, hard-core workout program, and pretty soon they looked like completely different women. The muscles that they weren't getting from the typical workout, they now had. Their diet was better; they had more energy. They needed a time commitment—sixty days—that was long enough to incorporate the change. At the end of the first sixty days, they took a week off, regrouped, then committed to another round. That's how much they liked the results of the buddy system. They helped each other achieve similar goals, and they challenged each other every day to step out of their comfort zones.

I trained a young swimmer named Micha Burden a few years ago. Her talents were above average, but her desire was a ten-plus. Micha—a five-foot-seven native of Anchorage, Alaska—was an athletic standout for the UC Berkeley Golden Bears, with whom she was an honorable mention all-American.

"My dad's always shared my goal of being an Olympian and being a professional athlete, and he said that he would support me after college, that I should give it a try," Micha said.

Micha began doing the work, but when people asked what she did, "I was completely embarrassed to tell them that I was training for the Olympics," she said. "My boyfriend would say, 'She's training for the Olympics,' and I wouldn't want to talk about it. Obviously, that's not really the best way to be successful."

When she described her desire to me for the first time, I could tell Micha was for real, but could she improve by eleven minutes—

enough to be competitive on the world stage? I tried my best to make it sound daunting enough to determine if her ambition was genuine and sustaining—just as her swim coach tried to do. She didn't fit the profile of an open water swimmer and we both knew it.

I made it clear that this was going to be incredibly difficult and that she would have to eat better, train better and think better.

I put together a training package that she could afford, and we started working together on the mental side of training. I helped her with visualization, self-talk and goal-setting.

"It was really nice to have someone that I could talk to just about all that stuff, about my goals and how I was training," she said. "Obviously, your swim coach is a great person to talk to about your training, but sometimes with everything else involved with being the best that you can be, it's just the training that takes focus, so it was nice to be able to bring in all the other aspects of trying to be your best with Ken."

We rewrote her Desire and Reward Statements and crafted a Personal Action Plan. Each time she rewrote her Desire Statement, it became more real and her excitement and enthusiasm grew, furthering her drive to maximize her potential and do everything that needed to be done, whether she wanted to or not. She rewrote her Desire Statement every day for seven days, and then we made it a goal.

Earlier, you thought about and wrote down your strengths and limitations. These are the strengths and limitations of a champion:

MICHA'S STRENGTHS
- Determination
- Hard worker
- Willingness to learn

- Humble
- Good technique
- High pain threshold
- Surrounded by great swimmers and solid coach

MICHA'S LIMITATIONS
- Petite
- Lack of experience
- Forced by economic circumstances to work a lot
- Had little money for the best food or international travel

For a year, Micha ate, thought and trained like a champion, with her eye on a U.S. Open Water World Championship in 2007. Nobody else gave her much of a chance, but I did. She visualized her race: finishing first!

After the race, she called me from Fort Myers, Florida, and said, "Guess what! I won the 10K!"

As planned, Micha beat the best open water swimmers in America and made the national team. Her bid for a spot on the Olympic team was unfortunately derailed when she broke a rib swimming in Brazil, interrupting her intensive training just before an important qualifying race.

With a clear, definite desire that becomes a goal and a personal action plan reflecting the most important things to work on, it will become apparent how you should spend your training time. Never underestimate yourself!

10

Mind Over Business in Action

You now have the mental tools needed to maximize your potential. The Mind Over Business program has given you a competitive advantage that will be with you for the rest of your working life. And there will be a carryover to other areas, as these techniques work well in school, sports and life. The key is to use them on a consistent basis and let your mind, body and actions work in harmony. Use the tools as designed and they will make your job easier.

It's time to reap the rewards of the time you've committed to the Mind Over Business program. Time to decide that you can see how it will work for you. Time to Finish Before You Start! You must do the exercises, because while reading them will give you awareness, actually practicing will give you the ultimate change and improvements you crave. Maybe you've read other books, and you haven't committed to them; this time, you need to see the program through!

One of the most valuable business decisions I ever made was

making up my mind to be a skilled communicator. For most of my life this was a foreign thought. Making a living as a public speaker, trainer and writer was a ridiculous notion for me. Besides being a high school dropout, I was a blue-collar worker and proud of it. Not selling, not speaking to groups—until then, I just let my hard work do my talking and it spoke pretty well.

After my introduction to the financial services industry, I immediately saw the value of the spoken word. The whole industry is built on conveying a message to the customer. My commitment was strong and my research intense. I read hundreds of books, listened to dozens of audio programs, went to seminars and workshops to educate myself on every conceivable area of human interaction.

I gave free speeches so I could practice. I recruited, hired and trained hundreds of people along the way, getting valuable feedback about success and failure from all. From scratch, I had to learn confidence, pronunciation, voice inflection, pitch, pace and power, how to craft a speech, how to listen, when to be assertive and how to use presence and posture to persuade an audience or command a room.

In the early part of my public speaking training, I rewrote an entire public speaking book, page by page, and word by word, with ink and paper, so I could really absorb the details of crafting a speech. After it was all said and done, I could remember specific instructions verbatim and how to apply them. This learned skill of memory visualization served me well, as I could give multiple forty-five-minute speeches or six-hour workshops with few or no notes. I could read a book and remember specific pages and paragraphs where I found interesting points or valuable research. My ability to remember was directly linked to how valuable the information was to me at the time and how I photographed or visualized the information. As a result of my growing desire, I would read a section and visualize immediately its importance or application.

This gave me the ability to construct a seminar, speech or sales presentation and remember and impart important, useable information. I can still remember my first paid speech, for the United Way. They paid me $400 to speak for an hour. I got up to give my presentation and did my performance cue and became somebody else. This appearance spun off many other speaking engagements and consulting jobs. For the first time in my life, I really loved learning, because it was what was needed to get me where I wanted to go.

This personal discovery snowballed into other areas as I was compelled to write three different books on three different subjects: sports, nutrition and business. And it continues to this day as I am constantly looking for new ways to improve my business skills and challenge myself in every way, constantly sharpening the blade and maintaining a fresh edge.

You, Too, Can Influence People

If you want to influence people, the number one thing you need is confidence. It doesn't matter what you look like, it doesn't matter how you talk—you must have confidence. Everything else is nice, but with just good looks, good speech and a great business plan, and no confidence, what do you have? A whole empty suit of nothing.

One of the best ways to influence people is to first influence yourself. Give yourself permission to be an unabashed self-promoter or product pitchman. A product or cause you believe in is paramount because if you don't believe in yourself or your product, you will fail.

Here's an example: Casey struggled after high school, drifting from one unskilled job to the next, marrying and divorcing young, never satisfied in any aspect of his life. A decent conversationalist, he eventually tried sales but found he couldn't influence people to make purchase decisions. In other words, Casey couldn't close the deal.

Casey heard me speak at a business seminar and figured that if an uneducated guy like me could influence people, so could he. He made his way through the crowd to talk to me personally. He was selling dental supplies at the time, something that failed to excite any passion in him. I told Casey to become a student of the profession. Subscribe to dental journals and read them. Speak the language of the industry. Feel confident before you get on the phone with sales prospects. See what success looks like before you meet a client face-to-face. Finish Before You Start: Experience the dentist buying your product and enjoy the experience before it ever happens. Today, Casey loves selling dental supplies. It provides a six-figure income and a flexible schedule that lets him enjoy his life.

People have a tendency to think confidence comes from success. How can you be successful if you are not confident? And what comes first—the chicken or the egg? Confidence is something we generate internally. It's a part of our self-esteem, and we develop confidence by the ways in which we think about ourselves, measuring our self-worth.

We have every reason to be confident in our goals, dreams and desires if we are semi-competent. So from where do we get confidence? It grows from how we think, talk to ourselves, see ourselves, and from our breathing and posture.

The following visualization exercise can turn a bad day into a good one, a scary situation into an exciting one and a shy person into one who is confident and strong.

〷〷〷〷〷〷〷〷〷〷〷〷 **E X E R C I S E** 〷〷〷〷〷〷〷〷〷〷〷〷

THE POSTURE OF CONFIDENCE

This exercise will help you become something you're not but need to be. And it will help you become whatever that is quickly.

Think about who in your own circle—or beyond it—displays an outward confidence and an inward strength. How would they enter a room? What expression would they have on their face? Notice their posture. Pretend to enter a room like they do. How does it feel? Consider your facial expressions and posture. Make it real, as if it's happening now. How do you breathe when in control? Think of a person you respect and admire and who gives a great speech or is an incredible salesperson. Notice how that person sounds. Listen to his or her voice inflection. Become aware of how that person controls the situation. What would happen if you could be more like that person? Notice how you would present. Does your voice sound confident and exude rapport with your audience? How do you make contact with the audience and draw them in? Feel as if you are this way now.

How to Influence People

We live in a highly competitive world where lots of people envy your job, sell what you sell and build what you build.

A sandwich shop owner is trying to influence office workers earning $10 an hour to buy a $6 sandwich. An insurance agent is trying to influence thirty-five-year-olds to spend $50 a month for a life insurance policy that will ultimately benefit someone else, because the buyer will be dead. A carpenter is trying to influence luxury buyers to hire him for a $40,000 kitchen remodel. A real estate agent is trying to influence empty nesters to buy a $1,000,000 home that was only worth $750,000 last year. A corporate middle manager is trying to positively influence hourly employees below her and executives above her. A long-term unemployed man is trying to influence potential employers to give him a chance and hire him over a thousand other applicants for the same position.

They all have a common goal: to influence a targeted individual who can reward them with what they want. Everybody is influencing or being influenced.

How can situations and jobs be so different yet so similar? The difference is in the day-to-day activity of the job or the search, and the similarity is that all these people are constantly attempting to influence others in the marketplace of ideas and services.

There is nothing more powerful when it comes to influencing others than belief. Beliefs can move mountains and cause people to act on the most illogical course of action.

Believe in yourself and believe in your product or service and you will be unstoppable. You will never let no stop you because you believe no is nothing more than one step closer to yes. It's a reality, not a myth. Sales is a numbers game. Even poor salespeople can make a good living if they see enough people. The biggest difference between a great salesperson and a poor one is that while great ones get fewer no's, they still get them. Great hitters still strike out and fail seven out of ten times! But the great ones have the ability to convey belief about what they are selling or promoting.

Establish Your Presence!

How important is presence?

- Would you rather buy a $5 sandwich from a slovenly dressed, dirty-looking food services worker or a $7 sandwich from a clean and neat preparer?
- Would you hire a carpenter who had good references but was late for the first appointment, couldn't look you in the eye and shook hands like a dead fish and said, "I think I can do it"? Or the one who was on time, with fewer references, and who shook with a firm grip, had good eye contact and said, "I know I can do it!"?
- What would make the best first impression: a financial planner who dressed casually, smelled like smoke and kept forgetting your name, or the one who was dressed in a professional manner, had an absence of any strong odor of any kind and took delight in remembering your name?
- Who would you rather hire? The candidate who seemed desperate, wore shoes scuffed and in need of polish and kept wiping the sweat from his forehead as he interviewed, or the one who seemed calm and confident, with shoes polished and a sweat-free forehead?

In each of these examples, the latter example is consistently the choice people make. Why? Because we make choices based on presence and often never find out that the one with less presence has more meat in his sandwich, or more substance in her experience, and is a better choice. Lack of presence keeps people from knowing your true value. Often we can't get past a poor first impression.

Be Assertive!

The difference between being pushy and coming across as obnoxious, assertive and professional is sometimes a fine line. It really comes down to how you say what you say and at times being creative in the way you say it.

I often attend the annual Manhattan Beach Open Volleyball Tournament, which is the Wimbledon of beach volleyball. The place is always packed, standing room only. One year, two ladies were searching for seats, and when they realized they were out of luck, they stayed at the front of the stands leaning against the guardrail to watch the game. The problem was that they were now blocking the view of others—myself included. After a few key points were played, people around me were grumbling, so I spoke up and said, "You ladies are gorgeous, and normally I would rather look at you than the game, but this is Manhattan and you will be much prettier when you step to the side." They turned and smiled, laughed and moved away. Everybody clapped, and you could hear a number of people say, "What a great way to do that."

In a business setting, sometimes being direct without anger is the best choice. You might tell a colleague, "That joke is inappropriate; please don't talk that way around me."

Be strong. Think before you speak—state the specific action you want others to take. Give directives you want others to take. Sometimes you need to be very direct—"I need you to finish this report by 3 p.m. on Friday so we can all go home on time."

Find Reasons to Believe in Yourself

Personal belief is the limit on how high you can rise, how much you can sell, how well you can lead. It's time to own the best belief system you can about yourself. Now is the time to solidify who you want to become and become that person.

You may find that others don't understand your change or see the need. It's kind of like going from being a meat eater to being a vegetarian; not all of your friends will easily embrace the change. If you announce it from the rooftops and try to convert the carnivores, they will resist. But if you quietly go about doing your thing—focusing on changing yourself—and they see a better, healthier you, they will eventually accept it and maybe even want to give it a try. The key is to change yourself without a lot of fanfare and bravado. Focus on you and your beliefs and what will make you more successful in business and in life.

Your personal beliefs shape who you are, and they have brought you to this very moment in your life. They shape your self-esteem and construct your values. It's easy to feel bad when you have negative beliefs about yourself. And it's just as easy to feel guilty when you're not living your true beliefs or core values. Not liking yourself and feeling guilty are sure ways to minimize your value and forever stay the same. To maximize performance and feel good about what you are doing, you first need to like yourself.

You would be surprised how many people don't like themselves. I'm not talking about self-loathing. It's more of a feeling of not being worthy. They don't think they are of value or deserve success: "Who am I that I should be more than I am?" or "It was good enough for my mom and it's good enough for me."

Some people have deep-seated feelings of failure or mediocrity.

They believe they are not smart enough, not well spoken enough or destined to a lousy fate. All they can remember is that they wasted their talent in high school, didn't do well in college or that first time they were passed over for promotion. I have had people tell me they were so used to failing or coming up short, why try anymore?

I did Mental Edge work with Natalie, a twenty-seven-year-old who was seriously disappointed about where she was in her life.

"I always fail," she told me. "Now I set my sights lower, or I don't establish goals anymore, so I am never disappointed."

She was once the MVP of her high school softball team and a first team all league, carried a solid 3.3 grade point average and scored a 1270 on the SATs. All that was enough to earn Natalie a four-year college scholarship. But because it wasn't a full ride to her dream school, she declared herself a failure. Once she was in college, the coach who recruited her nonetheless didn't support her, demonstrating that by the sparing way that he used her. When that coach left after Natalie's junior year, she became the recognized leader of the team and excelled on and off the field. But none of that mattered to Natalie; she viewed her college career as a failure because she "wasted the first three years."

She left school before graduation when her mother died and the pull of family obligations kept her from returning to finish. Natalie still had enough to offer an employer to land her dream job, but she viewed herself as a failure because she didn't get the degree.

You get the picture. Most of us would have been thrilled to achieve what this girl had done. Yet once she slipped into this downward spiral of negative, limiting beliefs, she couldn't rebound. In her mind, she couldn't match up to other people or their perceived expectations of her. Comparing to others can be a wonderful thing if it's a learning tool, but for validation, it's terrible!

There is always somebody, somewhere, getting better numbers or living larger. Have you ever noticed that the list of the world's Top 50 richest people is constantly changing? But can you imagine Bill Gates gauging his self-worth based on whether the list has him at number one or number eight?

Natalie was and is an overachiever. Coach after coach told her she was too small and wouldn't make it. She did more with less and succeeded beyond everyone else's expectations—just not her own.

The following is an exercise to deepen positive beliefs, and remove the shackles of the past.

‖‖‖‖‖‖‖‖‖‖‖‖‖‖‖‖‖‖‖‖‖‖‖ **EXERCISE** ‖‖‖‖‖‖‖‖‖‖‖‖‖‖‖‖‖‖‖‖‖‖‖‖‖‖‖‖‖‖‖

LEARN FROM THE PAST

‖‖‖

Write down what your life would be like right now if everything you have planned for or wanted was yours. What would you have right now?

———————————————————————————————————

———————————————————————————————————

What would you have had to do differently to have made that happen?

———————————————————————————————————

———————————————————————————————————

What beliefs would you have had to change?

_____

_____

Now write down what you want in your future. What kind of person do you want to be?

_____

_____

What do you want to have?

_____

_____

What beliefs do you need to change to make this happen?

_____

_____

Notice the similarities between the beliefs and actions that need or needed to change. Your old beliefs and actions caused you to come up short in the past and will cause you to come up short in your future. Often it's those same old beliefs that need changing in the present. If you don't change beliefs, your actions will not change and you will get the same frustrating results.

Now it's time to change your results. You are worthy of success and you have the capacity to do great things. But you must believe it to your core! To change fast, we will use the following sequence: Say it. See it. Feel it. Experience it.

The following exercise will help you to change quickly with the skillful use of Performance Talk.

|||||||||||||||||||||||||||||||||||||||||||||||||||||||||||||||||||||||||||||||||||||||||||||||||||||||||

||||||||||||||||||||||||||||||||||||||||| **E X E R C I S E** |||||||||||||||||||||||||||||||||||||||||||

CHANGE NOW FOR BETTER
|||||||||||||||||||||||||||||||||||||||||||||||||||||||||||||||||||||||||||||||||||||||||||||||||||||||||

Find a comfortable place where you will be without interruption and do your Instant Relaxation Technique (IRT). Breathe normally a few times and repeat the following, slowly, three times over: "Change is good, I am good, life is good." Next, picture what you look like having the life you want and being the person you want to be. Notice how you have learned from your past and your past is a valuable learning tool.

Allow a positive belief you have about yourself to pop into your head. What does life look like living this belief? How does it help you? What's another belief you have about yourself? What does this belief sound like as you are living it? What is your posture like? How does this belief help you? Think about a negative belief you have about yourself. How does it get in the way of your success? What irrefutable evidence do you have that you must believe this? None. What is another belief with which you can replace it?

What do you look like living this new belief? How do you use it in business? How does it get you closer to being who you want to be and having what you want to have? How do you talk to yourself when you believe this? Notice your tone of voice, your word choices. How do you feel when this belief is comfortable? Breathe normally and gently deep in the belly as you breathe in this new you.

Think about other beliefs you would like to shed and get rid of them now, like a dog sheds the old coat for the new. Push them away or dismiss them with "That's not for me." What will you embrace instead? What do you look like living these new beliefs? How do they affect your actions? How do you act in harmony with these new beliefs? Notice what comes into your life as a result of these changes. Notice all the benefits of these new beliefs, see them, feel them, and hear them.

Make up your mind right now to break the shackles of the past. See the chains fall as you raise your arms and embrace the beliefs that empower you. Conclude by repeating the following, three times over with passion and belief: "I'm worthy, capable and committed."

Now you are ready to use all the skills you already possess and apply all the skills you will learn to influence others and maximize your potential.

The Next 21 Days

The following 21-day action plan is a life changer. Committing to and implementing the learned techniques with the following habit-breakers will thrust you out of your comfort zone so you can fully live *Mind Over Business*. Your performance will improve and your energy will be off the charts. It's easy to follow and everyone can make a 21-day program work. You will be blasted out of your comfort zone and land firmly with a new attitude, perspective and appreciation for what you are capable of.

Surround yourself with an environment of excellence. Eliminate negative media. Do not watch the news or read a newspaper for twenty-one days. If you are taking a trip and weather is important, by all means check the weather, but that's it. The news in any form uses up valuable hours as it pounds negatives into your head. If something is truly important and you need to know it, I guarantee someone will inform you. This will save at least an hour a day and you will not waste any mental energy thinking about things of no value.

Listen to music that brings back positive memories, inspires you or puts a skip in your step. No tearjerkers or "life's a bummer" music. Stay away from talk radio—it's a time waster and fills your head with other people's agendas. It's often negative and petty. Listen one hour a day to a self- or business-improvement program.

Read a biography each week of someone you admire and pay attention to that person's actions.

Avoid negative people—even if they're family members. You know who these people are. Every business has one or more employees who complain about the boss, other people, or the economy and are nothing but downers. If you can't avoid them, redirect with a question, such as "What do you like about the boss?" or "What's the solution?" If they end up disliking you, count your blessings.

Talk yourself into effectiveness. Take one area of life or business that is getting in your way and write a Performance Talk for that challenge. If you are barely on time or often late, try "I take pride in being enthusiastic and early." Power through it every day for seven days, then write a new one. Tape it to your mirror and read it five times before bed every night in a calm manner and with as much imagery as you can. Read it again in the morning, five times, with as much passion and intensity as you can. Put one Performance Talk statement in your briefcase or purse and another in your car. Bombard yourself with Performance Talk and let the impact change you quickly.

Contemplate, meditate, clarify. Take five minutes a day to think about something you would like to achieve or become. It could be a little thing or your big goal or dream. First contemplate or think about what that something is. For example: "I want to be a better colleague." Meditate on becoming a better colleague and see yourself taking action to be a better colleague. The meditation will clarify how the new behavior fits in your life and help you find ways to incorporate it.

Another example: "I want to have more confidence." Think about specific situations and meditate on how to apply this new behavior, and this will clarify how the behavior impacts your goals and your life. Make sure your goals and meditations are specific and accurate. Sprinter Trevor James of Trinidad had the dream of being an Olympian. He set the goal, visualized success, and sure enough, he became an Olympian—and was still knocked out in the second round. He will tell you now his big regret was not setting the goal to medal. Although at a very deep level, he was still satisfied because he made his goal, Trevor, now a track and personal performance coach in Trinidad, makes sure all his athletes and clients are more precise.

Eat for performance. With all the energy drinks and concoctions on the market, you would think that everyone was functioning at a high level. *Wrong!* Energy drinks and concoctions that stimulate the nervous system or spike blood glucose set you up for a perpetual energy deficit, forever enslaving you like a ball and chain. Using stimulants, which is what coffee is, borrows tomorrow's energy for today, putting you in a vicious circle of depletion and stimulation.

The most energetic, happiest people I know don't use energy stimulants or do so on a rare basis. Energy stimulants also wreck havoc on emotions (how many people do you know who are crabby or unbearable until they have their morning coffee?) because of the blood sugar swings. Often, drinking a lot of water can stop the craving for caffeine. Drink water first thing in the morning, before you consume anything else. Drink water before each meal and more about an hour after dinner. This little trick alone will have you feeling better and will help you get off the stimulants.

Be careful of so-called natural energy drinks, as they may be just as damaging as anything else. Natural caffeine is still caffeine. Depending on how they're made and how much is in the drink, many natural ingredients are worthless. You are paying for caffeine, sugar and a few other ingredients that may not even work.

Here's a simple and easy meal profile that will help get your mind right as you improve your body:

Breakfast: Protein with a little fruit.

Mid-morning snack: Nuts or a small chunk of cheese and fruit (a few almonds and a plum).

Lunch: Grain-based carbs, protein, fat (example: tuna on toast).

Afternoon snack: Protein and veggies (2 ounces of turkey rolled up in lettuce) or nuts and veggies (6 walnut halves and 2–3 carrot sticks). You can also eat about 150 calories of a high-protein bar. Builder and Balance bars are good choices.

Dinner: 4–6 ounces of lean protein, a large salad with olive oil–based dressing, and vegetables—no potato, pasta or grains except once a week.

Also, eat fast food only once a week—or *never*. Eat red meat no more than twice a week. No evening snacks. If you just have to eat something, choose 150 calories of protein with little or no carbohydrates. Alcohol? No more than once a week.

After the first week, your energy will be up, your brain will be clear. It's also the time to give up smoking.

Log on to BioDynamax.com for more specific information for your body type and metabolism.

Do something new. Drive a new route to work today. Shop at a different store tomorrow; shop the usual store rows in a different order. Change your hairstyle next week or modify your look in some other way. Yes, the 1980s are over—bring your look to the twenty-first century!

Start a new workout routine or try something you have always wanted to do. Take guitar, dance or karate lessons. Make it something challenging and fun you have always wanted to do. Sleep on the other side of the bed. Get to work five minutes earlier and go right to priority one.

Prioritize daily. Do the do! Before you leave your workplace, make a to-do list of all you need to do the next day. Prioritize the bottom line first. Be careful of fillers that take time and keep you from doing the right thing at the right time. Every time you accomplish something on the list, cross it off and then—and only then—go to the next one.

Move it or lose it. Your body is your most valuable asset. Take care of it and it will serve you well. If you want energy, you must expend energy. It's the most remarkable thing to watch Dr. Mark Song, who is in his fifties, compete in Ironman Triathlons. He is an emergency room doctor who trains every day, surfs, spends time with his family and has boundless energy. He knows the body works best when you combine muscle-building activity with aerobic activity. So if you are a walker or runner, add resistance training, and if you are an avid weight lifter, add something aerobic: cycle, run or walk. If you are just starting out, split your time evenly between strength building and aerobic activity. Train five times a week. Don't be sucked in by gimmicks.

Put it off no more. Once a week, tackle something you have been putting off. Clean that garage, organize your office or get those taxes done. It feels so good to do what needs to be done, even when it's not your favorite thing to do. Winners do what needs to be done whether they want to or not.

Finish Before You Start. Experience what you want to be like after twenty-one days. See yourself doing the 21-day challenge and enjoying the process. Feel the abundant energy and clear thinking as you take a quantum leap in attitude and actions. Rewrite your Desire Statement every day for seven days and then once a week for the final two weeks. Write it first as "I want to" and then, when you're ready to commit, write the statement as "I will."

Make up your mind you will start and finish this 21-day challenge. Sometime between Day 1 and Day 21 you will feel like a cloud has been lifted; your energy will be high and your thinking will be clear.

|||||||||||||||||||||||||||||||||||||||||| **E X E R C I S E** ||||||||||||||||||||||||||||||||||||||||||||||||||

START CHANGE *NOW*
||||||||||||||||||||||||||||||||||||||||||||||||||||||||||||||||||||||||||||||||||||||||||||||||||

All of us work for someone or have our own business. The following exercise will help you start down the path to getting more satisfaction out of your job.

How can you view your current job more positively?

It gives me _____

What three daily work activities can you change to be more productive?

I will change, add or subtract these three activities (examples: earlier start time, improve focus, walk during lunch):

1. _____

2. _____

3. _____

How can you change your physical environment to be more positive? (Examples: bring in new pictures, rearrange your desk, paint the wall a fun color.)

I will change the following:

1. _____

2. _____

3. _____

How can you wrap yourself in a mental environment of excellence?

I will incorporate the following thoughts about my colleagues, supervisors and myself:

Colleagues: _____

Supervisors: _____

Self: _____

Web Tip: Meetup.com

Here's a great way to meet people who share your passion for a career, lifestyle, hobby or anything else. It's called Meetup and it's a free way to find like-minded folks in your community. According to the site, more than two thousand groups get together in communities each day "with the goal of improving themselves or their communities." Check it out at Meetup.com.

Be Ready. Your Future Self Will Be Amazing!

Your mind needs to be made up to be successful at whatever business you choose. The Mind Over Business program is logical and user-friendly: contemplate, meditate and clarify. These three steps clarify for right actions and maximum productivity, as you know exactly what you want and how best you use your time.

Your new perceptions are empowering, changing you from the inside out. Negative beliefs are eliminated as you carve out limiting habits and thoughts, replacing them with an "I can" attitude and the actions of an achiever.

Your breathing coordinates your mind, body and actions to be in harmony with what you truly want. You use your past, good or bad, as a springboard to a better future, never blaming anyone for your lot in life.

"If it is to be, it's up to me" is more than a saying, it's a way of life. Your posture, facial expressions and deepest thoughts reflect a person content yet growing in knowledge and wisdom as you continually challenge yourself to be the best you can be, all the while knowing happiness is not just for high achievers.

True success is not about titles or money, but about living life on your terms, being your authentic self and living in accord with your higher values. This powerful tool you now possess called visualization is much more than just pretty pictures; it's also a learning tool, a facilitator of change opening up a world of possibilities. With CRA, you have tremendous power to live the life of your dreams. It's not always going to be easy, because life happens. But with the mental skills you have learned from this book, you will be prepared for anything that comes your way. No matter how difficult a challenge may be, you will fight through it and come out the other side a better person.

I expect everyone applying these techniques to be more successful in business and happier in life. Many of you will go on to greatness. Some will break free of jobs you took just to get by, and the drudgery that goes with that, to live your dreams. You have tremendous potential just waiting to break out, and *Mind Over Business* smashes the pattern of mediocrity.

Onward and upward; your best is yet to come.

ABOUT THE AUTHORS

Ken Baum is one of the premier sports performance psychologists in the world. He is owner of BioDynamax Training Center in Orange County, California, a training center for Olympic-caliber athletes and business leaders. His experience is as diverse as his client list because athletes from around the world seek out his training.

He conducts dozens of public and private seminars annually throughout the world and teaches thousands of people a year how to improve sports and business performance. He is rated as one of the most powerful and entertaining motivational speakers in America and has shared the stage with some of the biggest names in sports, entertainment and politics, including Phil Jackson, Terry Bradshaw, John Wooden, Larry King, Bob Dole, Naomi Judd, Suzy Orman, Donovan McNabb, Randy Johnson and many more.

Baum's clients from the business and sports world have included staff from financial giants such as Merrill Lynch and E. F. Hutton, the *Omaha World Herald* newspaper and more than two hundred other companies, as well as major sports stars, such as the gold medal–winning U.S. men's Olympic volleyball team, figure skater Sasha Cohen, Tampa Bay Rays baseball player Carlos Pena—winner of the 2007 Comeback of the Year Award and the 2007 Silver Slugger Award, one of only two players to ever win both in the same year—and Bobsled World Champions Steven Holcomb and Steve Mesler, to name a few.

Baum is the author of *The Mental Edge: Maximize Your Sports Potential with the Mind–Body Connection* (Perigee, 1999), *Metabolize: The Personalized Program for Weight Loss* (Putnam/Perigee, 2000) and *The Performance Zone* (audiobook; Nightingale/Conant, 2000) and has appeared in or written articles for *Volleyball Monthly*, *Men's Journal* and *Sports Illustrated for Women*.

As a lifetime athlete and business owner, Baum practices the Mental Edge exercises daily as he faces life's challenges with a positive, solution-based attitude, passing this on to his karate and mixed martial arts students. When not training others or minding the business, he trains himself in martial arts, rock climbing, hiking, fly-fishing, surfing, weight lifting and running.

Bob Andelman lives in St. Petersburg, Florida, with his wife and daughter. He is the author or coauthor of several bestselling biographical, business, management and sports books, including:

- *The Profiler* (Hyperion Voice) with Pat Brown
- *Will Eisner: A Spirited Life* (Dark Horse/M Press, www.aspiritedlife. com)
- *The Profit Zone: Lessons of Strategic Genius from the People Who Created the World's Most Valued Companies* (Times Books/Random House), with Adrian Slywotzky and David Morrison
- *Built from Scratch: How a Couple of Regular Guys Grew the Home Depot from Nothing to $30 Billion* (Times Books/Random House), with Bernie Marcus and Arthur Blank
- *Mean Business: How I Save Bad Companies and Make Good Companies Great* (Times Books/Random House), with Albert J. Dunlap
- *The Consulate: An Agent Wyckoff Mystery* (MIHI Advisory Group), with Thomas Stutler

Andelman also produces and hosts the extremely popular "Mr. Media Interviews," an online celebrity and media interview radio and TV show distributed on his website, www.mrmedia.com.

For more information on the *Mind Over Business* program, Mental Edge certification or inviting Ken Baum as a speaker at your next event, please go to MindOverBusiness.com. While you're there, get a free audio download of Ken Baum's "Mental Edge Minute."

For more information on being your best and living Mind Over Business, including free audio downloads, Ken Baum's "Mental Edge Minute" podcast, audio and DVD programs, workshops, certifications, consulting, or having Ken speak at your next corporate event, contact Biodynamax at the website and phone numbers below.

When you are ready to take it to the next level, attend a Mind Over Business Multiday Boot Camp and watch your energy, happiness and productivity soar!

Business owners, executives and managers, get more out of yourself and others with Mind Over Business Professional Certification. This dynamic program will give you the skills you need to take everyone to the next level.

MindOverBusiness.com
800-828-EDGE

Get the tools you need to transform your body as well as your mind with Ken Baum's Performance Zone Nutrition Program for Weight Loss and Energy designed for your unique metabolism.

Biodynamax.com